*A Word in Your Ear*

*By the same author from Four Courts Press*

A Dictionary of Anglo-Irish: Words and Phrases from Gaelic
   in the English of Ireland

The Words We Use

The Dialect of Forth and Bargy (*with T.P. Dolan*)

# A Word in Your Ear

DIARMAID Ó MUIRITHE

FOUR COURTS PRESS

Set in 11 on 13 Bembo
and published by
FOUR COURTS PRESS LTD
Fumbally Lane, Dublin 8, Ireland
e-mail: info@four-courts-press.ie
*and in North America by*
FOUR COURTS PRESS
c/o ISBS 5804 NE Hassalo Street, Portland, OR 97213.

ACKNOWLEDGEMENT

These articles are reproduced from the *Irish Times*,
by kind permission of the Editor.

A catalogue record for this title
is available from the British Library.

ISBN 1-85182-339-5

Printed in Ireland
by ColourBooks Ltd, Dublin.

*For Antonio González-Guerrero*

'You must get into the habit of looking intensely at words ... Never let a word escape you that looks suspicious. It is severe work; but you will find it, even at first, interesting, and at last, endlessly amusing.'

*Ruskin*

# Contents

## Whitherate —Feck —Gandermonth

Madge McQuaid, who lives in Bettyglen, Raheny, has sent me some very interesting words. One of these is *whitherate*, noun, a torment, nuisance.

The suffix *-ate* (from Latin *atus*, past participal ending of verbs that end in *-are*) in the sense of the product of a process, is rare enough even in the literary language. *Condensate*, a product of condensation, is one example.

*Whither* is found in England's northern shires and in Scotland and, as far as I know, has not previously been recorded in Ireland.

It takes various forms, *quhidder* and *wuther* among them. *Whitherate*, noun, is not recorded in the EDD, but it does give the following: '*whither* etc. A gust of wind, the noise caused by a rushing, violent movement, a violent hurry.' It also gives *whither*, verb, to tremble, shake; of the wind, to bluster, rage. Miss Emily Brontë, in *Wuthering Heights*, kindly gave the following help: "Wuthering Heights" is the name of Mr Heathcliff's dwelling, "wuthering" being a significant provincial adjective, descriptive of the atmospheric tumult to which its station is exposed in stormy weather.' From these to Madge McQuaid's word for torment is a small step.

The verb *to feck*, to steal, is taking the night's sleep from J. O'Meara in Limerick city.

This verb is more common in Ireland than elsewhere, it seems. Joyce has 'They had fecked cash out of the rector's room' in the *Portrait,* and mentions 'fecking matches from counters' in *Ulysses*. Where this slang word came from is another matter. Oxford says it doesn't know its origin.

May I modestly suggest that the word may be related to the colloquial German *fegen*, to plunder, from *fegen*, to sweep?

Finally, an absolute beauty from a lady who signs herself 'Ringsend Woman'. This good lady has lived in London for sixty years; she left Dublin when she was twenty. 'When my world was young,' she writes, 'you'd hear the old women in Ringsend say about a man seen staggering home from the pub every night while his wife was above in Holles Street having another babby for him,

"He's enjoying his gander month." Why gander? I have often wondered about it.'

Probably from the gander's aimless-looking walk, while the goose sits hatching. The expression is very old. Thomas Dekker used it in 1636 in one of his plays: 'Is't gander moneth with him?' And it may have been centuries older than the bould Thomas's day. Dear Ringsend Woman, please tell me who you are.

## Ulster Scots

The cocks have been crowing loudly on Ulster's linguistic middens for about a year now. From one side we are told – only by its lunatic fringe, I must say – that Ulster Scots is a pure speech, untainted by Irish. This, of course, is nonsense. The immigrants from the Highlands and from Galloway and Ayrshire brought with them a substantial vocabulary of Gaelic words. From the other side we heard crows of acclamation for the EU experts who recently refused to recommend that money be paid to help Ulster Scots survive. 'A dialect of a dialect!', wrote one ass, who doesn't even know that Scots is a language, not a dialect of English.

Ulster Scots deserves to be cherished, whatever the EU 'experts' might think. You'll find the pockets it survives in, from Down right around to Donegal and as far south as Monaghan, listed in an essay the late Brendan Adams contributed to *The English Language in Ireland,* a book of Thomas Davis Lectures which I edited for RTÉ some years ago. This language is more archaic than any variety of Scots you'll hear in Scotland; and you should know that if you drive up into the glens above Cullybackey in west Antrim, for example, those gentle people will address you in Ulster Hiberno-English for your own comfort, and will speak braid Scots among themselves.

Here's a sample of their speech collected by Brendan Adams not so long ago near Cullybackey. A widower, a bottle of whiskey in his pocket, has a mishap on his journey to view another woman.

'The next thang A knowed ma yann (*one*) fit (*foot*) slapped (*slipped*) ann (*in*) behann the athar yann an doon A went aan ma groof (*belly*) ann the coo shairn (*shit*). That wasnae aa. Wheen a spraaghled (*sprawled*) aboot traayin tae get up, shae (*shoe*) nor fit cud A putt undher me. At laast A gaut on ma baakside an airsed ower tae A gaut o haul (*hold*) o yann o thos pailin posts forninst the lannt (*flax*) daam. A was chaakin (*shaking*) wae the coul, an claarried (*smeared*) wae coo dung frae heel tae thraaple (*throat*). A thoght Raab wud navver come. At last A hard his wheeple (*whistle*) ann the whuns (*whins*). 'Jammie, is thaat you?' Sez aai: 'Whaa dae ye thank it wud be? A hae broke ma leg.' 'Naw,' sez he. 'Is the whusky aa raght?'


## Gallivanting – Dub – Fowt – Foo – Gombeen

'Is the word *gallivanting* very old?' asks a man born and bred in London's Boswell Street. His name is John Chang and he was introduced to this column by his Irish girlfriend.

How old *gallivanting* is I'm not sure. It was first seen in print in 1824, in a book by W.H. Pyne called *Wine and Walnuts*, but it may have been around the streets long before that.

In the 19th century it became quite an 'in' word, thanks to Thackeray. It then meant, as it means today, to gad about seeking pleasure; it also meant to flirt, an occupation one can pursue without gadding, I'm told. Pyne's hero, for example, was 'sitting at his ease gallivanting with a publican's daughter'.

Origin? Oxford thinks that it may be a humorous perversion of *gallant*. There is a French dialect word, *galvauder*, and the American *World Books Dictionary* asks us to consider this.

*Dub* is an old Fanad word for a pool of rainwater, Mary Mac-Loughlin tells me. It was her granny's word.

An old word this, found in Scotland as well as in the north of this blessed isle. Tyrone's Carleton wrote of 'the dub before the door' in *Fardorougha the Miser*, and Burns has: 'O ye wha leave the springs of Calvin For gumlie dubs of your ain delvin.'

The Scots also have the marvellous *dub-skelper*. To skelp in this case means to trod heavily, to splash, so that a dub-skelper is a person who doesn't care where he walks and by figurative extension, one of those who spakes his mind, and who doesn't care who's listenin'. A bosthoon. Anyway, Mary's *dub* is from Low German *dobbe, a* pool of stagnant water.

From Great Yarmouth comes a letter from J.H. Franklin, who asks me to throw some light on the word *fowt*, an idiot. Gross's dictionary of 1790 has it, spelt *fout:* 'An expression of contempt.' A Great Yarmouth man won't be surprised that the word came from Scandinavia originally. The Old Norse was *fauti*, a fatuous man.

The Yorkshire word shouldn't be confused with the Ulster *fout*, a spoiled child, a pet. This is a Scots import and an old word it is. Barbour used it in his *Bruce*, back in 1375. Old French *folet*.

Finally, in answer to many letter, *gombeen* is from Irish *gaimbín*, interest on a loan, from Middle English *cambie*, barter, exchange, from medieval Latin *cambium*, from a Celtic word tentatively identified by Whitley Stokes as *kmbion*.

## Words from Devon and Cornwall

An interesting letter arrived recently from Canon Brian Lougheed, of St Mary's Rectory, Ballycasheen, Co. Kerry. The word *finagle* is bothering him. A friend of his used the word as he would himself; to both it means to achieve something against the odds, as in making a contract in bridge that one really doesn't deserve.

Webster was consulted, and to the canon's surprise the word has been given the meaning 'to obtain by guile or swindling'.

Finagle, I was myself surprised to find, is 20th-century American. It is a variant of a much older word still used in Dorset, Devon and Cornwall, and also in Gloucestershire. Collins says that finagle is an informal word, and that it means to get or achieve by trickery, craftiness or persuasion and in all the great dictionaries the word carries the whiff of deceit.

At any rate, the older word from which finagle comes is *fainaigue*. There are, however, quite a number of variants to be found in the dialect glossaries of England, *feneage, finague, furnaig* and *venaig* among them.

It means (1) to revoke at cards, to renege; (2) to fail of a promise, to play truant, to shirk work. *Notes and Queries* for 1854 has, from Cornwall: 'Most frequently applied to cases where a man has shown appearances of courtship to a woman and then left her without any apparent reason. (3) To deceive by flattery; to obtain by improper means, to cheat.'

From Cornwall again, there is a couplet that goes: 'But a maiden came one day and feneagued his heart away.' Its origin? Probably Old French *fornier,* to deny somebody or something – God, a charge, for instance (modern *nier, denier*), this from Latin *foris*, from abroad, and *negare*, to deny, I think.

James Maher from Tipperary wants to know where the expression the *back of God-speed* comes from. The *God-speed* was a screen placed in front of the door of a house to keep off the wind. Hence the expression came to mean an unfrequented place that nobody wants to visit.

God is found in many interesting expressions. *God's child* is the Sussex term for a mentally handicapped person, their equivalent of our *duine le Dia. God-forgive-me* is a jug used for heating ale. You'll still see them hanging in old Dorset pubs. Hardy mentions them in *Far from the Madding Crowd.*


## Snuck – Flisk – Eye-fiddle

Angela M'Ginn from Ballynamoney, Carrick-on-Shannon, tells me that her husband, a wildfowler, uses the expression, 'I snuck up on a bird'; she wants to know where this *snuck* originated. In America, where it became current not earlier than the turn of the present century. It's a solecistic past tense of the standard *sneak*; an American mistake, if you like. That's all there's to it, Angela.

From Pamela Lang, a Scot who has settled down in Belfast, comes a query about two words. The first is *flisk*. Her Galloway aunt used to say, 'Go on, flisk off out', when she wanted to get the kids out from under her feet.

The dialect dictionaries have recorded this word in Scotland,

Ireland and England. It seems to be related to both *whisk* and *flick* and the EDD glosses it as 'to whisk, move quickly from place to place; to frisk, leap, bounce; of a horse: to be restive'. Scott in *Guy Mannering* (1815) has: 'While that langlugged limmer o' a lass is gaun flisking in an out o' the room.' Hence we have *flisky*, skittish, restive, recorded by Patterson in Antrim and Down, 'specially applied to a mare which kicks when touched on the flanks'. Flisk is an imitative word.

I wonder had Pamela's aunt two cognate words from Galloway, *fliskmayhoy* and *fliskmahaigo*. Both mean a foolish, giddy girl, a flirt. Scott has 'That foolish fliskmahoy, Jenny Rintherout' in *Antiquaries*; he also refers to 'fliskmahaigo chit-chat'.

Pamela's other word is *flit*, to move from one house to another, and her query is about the word's origin. Flit is from Old Norse *flytja*, to cause to move; to migrate.

*Eye-fiddle*, in some places called *high-fiddle*, is a mummer's or a wrenboy's mask. Thomas Phelan of Kilkenny and John O'Brien of Limerick wrote to ask about the expression's origin.

It's a corruption of Irish *aghaidh fidil*, literally fiddle-face, because it often resembles a fiddle in being long-faced. In northern England a fiddle-face is a person with a doleful, lugubrious expression on his or her puss. Part of a Tyrone mummer's rhyme goes: 'Here I come Fiddly Funny. I'm the man collects the money. All silver and no brass! Bad money won't pass!' Thanks to Séamas Ó Catháin for that.

## Scaldy – Mind – Beef

The dialect word *scaldy*, an unfledged bird, has, I see, been the subject of two letters to the Editor. The word is not of Irish origin, and the Irish *scalltán* and the Scots *scaldachan* come from the same source – the Old Norse *skalli*, a baldhead.

All this tally-ho about mad cow disease has led J. Aspel of Waterford to write enquiring about the origin of the phrase *Where's the beef?* This is often attributed to Walter Mondale, who famously used it when questioning the merits of his opponent, Gary Hart's policies, in the fight for the Democratic party's presidential nomination. Mondale, however, was using a well-known television advertisement for Wendy's hamburger chain. This showed three oul wans inspecting a tiny slice of meat in an enormous bun – the product of a rival chain, of course. The first woman said: 'It sure is a big bun.' The second agreed: 'It sure is a big fluffy bun.' But the third one added: 'Yea, but where's the beef?'

Are you confused about this beef scare? Was Sir Andrew Aguecheek right when he remarked to Toby Belch: 'Methinks sometimes I have no more wit than a Christian or an ordinary man has: but I am a great eater of beef and I believe that does harm to my wit'? He had a drop taken, of course, when he said that.


'When I was in school in the south, I was constantly corrected when I said or wrote "I mind" instead of "I remember",' Ann F. from Newry tells me. 'Was my English teacher right? It was, she said, merely local speech and not found in literature.'

Merely local speech, eh? *Mind* has a distinguished pedigree. Not found in literature? Scot has 'Hout, tout, man, mind where the Stuarts come frae.' Burns has 'He forgets his loves and debts An' minds his griefs no more.' 'I can mind him ever since I was growing up a hard boychap,' wrote Thomas Hardy in *Under the Greenwood Tree.* Jane Barlow used it in her Ulster writings, as did Lyttle, Moira O'Neill, Seumus MacManus and God only knows how many more. The word is from Old English *myndgian, to* remember, bear in mind.


## Slaves – Slav – Franks – Roués


'There are cases in which more knowledge of more value may be conveyed by the history of a word than by the history of a campaign.' So wrote Coleridge.

Take the word *slave.* Gibbon, in *Decline and Fall,* has this to say about the word: 'The martial superiority of the Teutonic races enabled them to keep their slave markets supplied with captives taken from the Slavonic tribes. Hence, in all the languages of

Western Europe, the once glorious name of Slave has come to express the most degraded condition of men. What centuries of violence and warfare does the history of this word disclose.'

Gibbon was probably wrong in thinking that the idea of 'glory' was implied in the national name of Slav. It is generally held now that the Slavs gave themselves this name as being 'the intelligible', or 'the people who speak intelligibly'. This idea of linguistic superiority is common enough; many races regard their strange-speaking neighbours as 'barbarian', that is, 'stammering', or even 'dumb'. Barbarian comes originally, through Latin and Greek, from Sanskrit *barbara,* stammering.

Archbishop Chenevix Trench of Dublin associated the word *frank,* through medieval Latin, *francus,* free, with the Franks, 'honourably distinguished from the Gauls and degenerate Romans among whom they established themselves by their independence, their love of freedom, their scorn of a lie'. *Frank* is derived from a lost Old High German word for a spear or javelin, a relative of Anglo-Saxon *franca* and Icelandic *frakka.*

Trench has a note on *roué,* 'a word which throws light on a shameful page of French history'. *Roué* is properly and primarily one broken on a wheel. Its present and secondary meaning is derived from that Duke of Orleans who was regent of France after the death of Louis XIV. It was his ambition to gather around him companions worse, if possible, and wickeder than himself. These he called his roués. The roués themselves said that the word expressed rather their readiness to give any proof of their loyalty to their master, even to suffer the tortures of the wheel, then reserved for the worst malefactors.

Emerson called words 'fossil poetry'. Trench was right when he said that they could be called fossil history as well.


## Mother Bunch – Aloof


In certain English public houses, especially those which cater for sailors home from the sea, some very old slang terms have survived for centuries. The hostess of a pub in Cornwall which I recently graced with my presence, asked me whether I wanted *Mother Bunch* with my whiskey. Thinking this was some kind of month-old Cornish delicacy of the pastie variety I declined, and asked the lady for water. 'Mother Bunch *is* water, love', she explained graciously.

She could throw no light on the origin of the term, but assured me that it was common in far-off Greenwich, where she was reared. Rhyming slang, I thought, and we both spent a pleasant interlude guessing and jumping to the wrong conclusions.

Eric Partridge has since informed me that it is not rhyming slang at all, and that furthermore it was in common use in taverns frequented by Marlowe and Dekker. In the latter's *The Shoemaker's Holiday*, performed in 1599, we find: 'Am I sure that Paul's steeple is a handful higher than London Stone, or that the Pissing-Conduit leaks nothing but pure Mother Bunch? Am I sure that I am lusty Firk? God's nails, do you think that I am so base to gull you?'

Mother Bunch was a well-known alehouse hostess, and is mentioned in *Pasquil's Jests* in 1604.

*Aloof* is an old word whose origins may also lie in taverns much older than the Mermaid. It is *a* + *loof*, and loof, now obsolete, was a form of *luff*, a word still in use among sailors. Luff, apart from meaning the forward edge of a fore-and-aft sail, and the fullest and broadest part of a ship's bow, means that act of turning the bow of a ship towards the wind, a manoeuvre often performed so that she can draw apart from other craft. Thus *a-luff*, and *aloof* have come to mean 'one who stands apart'.

*Luff* comes from a piece of equipment which helped to accomplish the aforementioned manoeuvre. It was known in Old French as *lof*, and in Middle Dutch as *loef*, the peg of the tiller. Collins asks us to compare Old High German *laffa*, the palm of the hand, an oar blade; and the Russian *lapal*, paw. It might also have mentioned the Irish *lapa* which, apart from meaning a paw, means a flipper.

Intriguing, this etymological game, isn't it?

# Guys – Glib – Dunnage

A correspondent, Mary O'Brien of Limerick, gets annoyed with an American female friend who addresses other women as guys. 'I can't get it into her head that this usage of hers is incorrect; Guy Fawkes wasn't a woman.'

Ah, but the American guy, as in 'good guy', has nothing to do with old Guido Fawkes. There was an earlier guy, a leader, a support. Hence guy-rope. Guy in the American sense was first used by Dunbar in his fine poem on London, 'the flour of Cities all'. In one verse he praises the Lord Mayor: 'No Lord of Parys, Venyce, or Floraunce In dignitye or honour goeth to him nigh He is exampler, loode-star, and guye.' And had the first citizen been a woman, Dunbar would still have called her a guy. From Old French *guie*, from *guier*, to guide.

One of the words given to me by the late Brendan Adams, who did so much for Ulster lexicography, was *glib*, used in its old sense of slippery or smooth in Co. Down. M.J. Brown of Dundonald asks if we've got the word in the south.

I must say that I've never come across it. Browning has the good line, 'The snow lies glib as glass and cold as steel.'

John Clare has 'Smooth as glass the glibbed pool is froze.' Shakespeare confined it to people, 'glib and slippery creatures' in *Timon*. I would guess that the metaphorical usage has by now taken over from the old simple meaning of the word, except in places where old words are conserved and cherished, like Down and Antrim.

An Antrim man recently sent me the word *dunnage*. It is found in southern England as well as in Antrim, and there too it means odds and ends; baggage, clothes etc. In the London of the last century dunnage meant a tool-basket and other things carried in a parcel on their backs by navvies and labourers. It was originally a technical term for the light material, such as brushwood, mats and the like, stowed among the cargo of a vessel in the days of the square-riggers, to keep it from being injured in a storm. I first heard the word, and the explanation, from an old sailor called

Henry Browne, who lived in Sugarhouse Lane, New Ross. He would have been glad to know, God rest him, that Oxford confirmed his gloss.

Apropos of this, Mr Chalmers Trench of Killrian, Slane, Co. Meath, has written to me: '*Dunnage* is, or was, in common use in the milling fraternity. Specifically, I heard it in the oatmeal and provender mills of Drogheda, when they were still in operation up to the 1960s, and before the regular use of wooden pallets. The word then meant loose boards on which bags of meal would be placed to keep them off the floor and allow a circulation of air. That is an additional meaning to those given in the OED, though it is very similar to the use of dunnage to protect a ship's cargo. I thought this might be worth recording.'

It is indeed, and I've sent it to Oxford to keep Killrian on the linguistic map.

## Toly – Chavel

Mary Madden wrote from Toomebridge, Co. Antrim, about a word, *toly*, used by her aunt and cousins forty years ago. Her daughter wrote from Paris asking her to ask yours truly about the matter. In Antrim, *toly* meant baker's dough.

I'm sure this is the same word as *toalie*, a Scottish word for a small round bannock or cake of any kind of bread, according to the EDD, which also states that the word was obsolete in Scotland by 1900.

Mrs Madden's mother also used the word *chavelled* for anything that was roughly cut at the edges. This word puzzles her as well. A very old word this, common in Yorkshire, where it means to chew slowly and imperfectly; to gnaw, to tear with the teeth. A Yorkshire man was heard to complain: 'Look how oor coo's chavvel'd my cap.' In the same part of England a horse is said to chavel when biting his bit. Hence they have 1. *chavelings*, the fragments of what has been gnawed or nibbled, husks and refuse left by rats and mice. 2. *chavvlement*, a mass of pulpy, gnawed matter. The oldest reference to the word in literature is in Gervase Markham's *Masterpiece* of 1610: 'He doth, as it were, chavell or chaw a little hay.' The word is from the Middle English *chauel*, jaw; Old English *ceafl*. I'm glad to know it survives in Toomebridge.

## Gang – More Mill Words

The verb *gang*, go, is the subject of a letter from M. McCann of Lurgan. This word is to be found all over Scotland, northern England and the north of Ireland. A Scots rhyme goes: 'Wild geese, wild geese, ganging to the sea, Good weather it will be. Wild geese, wild geese, ganging to the hill, The weather it will spill.' The word is from Old English *gangan*, and in its present form is as old as the York Plays of *c.*1400. Ferguson in his 1641 *Proverbs* has, 'He gangs early to steal that cannot say na.' We Southerners don't have *gang*, and consequently have missed out on a number of interesting related words. *Ganging* means moving, stirring, active, in working order; hence *ganging*, the furnishing of a mill, which the tenant was bound to uphold. *Ganging man* means a tramp in Burns country.

To gang also meant to walk, to travel on foot. 'Bairns maun creep e'er they gang' is in Henderson's *Proverbs* (1832). 'Are ye gangin' or have you the car?', asked a Yorkshire friend of mine recently. From this gang came *gangway,* and the Antrim expression 'gang doon the house', meaning go down to the parlour.

*Gang* also means a gait, style of walking; pace. 'He has a good gang' means he walks at a good pace. Children use *gang* as a noun meaning turn, spell: 'It's your gang noo.' *Gang* also means a freight of water carried from a well, and this is often used in another sense: 'Many a gang I carried frae her well' means just what you think it does.

Chalmers Trench's recent letter about *dunnage* prompted Jane Kennedy from Bangor to enquire about the northern millword *flowan,* dust. Canon Noel Jackson of Craigavon last year sent me an equivalent, *stour,* in the south I've heard *dannock* (Irish *deannach*). Patterson in his Glossary of Down and Antrim words (1890) has *flowan:* 'the light clinging dust in a flax-scutching mill; small segments of the flax stem'.

The *Ballymena Observer* (1892) brought the word from the mill to the house: 'light, material-like threads or hair with dust attached, blowing about especially through a house that is not regularly dusted.' The EDD has another Irish *flowan*: bog-cotton. Its origin? The EDD has nothing to say; I'd guess Old English *flowan*, related to Old Norse *floa*, Greek *plein*, to float, and Sanskrit *plavate*, he swims.

## Scuddler – Swope – Trawly

Mary McClafferty sends me a good word from Derry, a word I myself have heard many times in Donegal. Mary spells it *scoodler* and she says that it means a young person who helps out in the kitchen, drawing water from the pump in the yard, cleaning out after an incursion of hens, laying the table, and so on. My wife, who is a Donegal woman, uses the word as a term of endearment for a youngster.

The new Concise Ulster Dictionary has *scuddler*, 'a young servant boy', from Scots 'a kitchen boy' from Old French *esculier,* and an unattested hypothetical form, not found in the historical record, *escudeler*. Fair enough; but we find much nearer home the Scots Gaelic *sguidilear*, pronounced *scoojiler*, Malcolm MacLennan's dictionary tells us: a scullion, drudge; a mean fellow.

The Surrey farmer at the National Ploughing Championship, who, like myself had escaped the rain by making for a hospitality tent, said that it was 'comin' down in treddles' as we listened to it drumming on our canvas roof. God rest my old friends, Maggie Whitty from Horeswood in south Wexford, and Paddy Doyle, who came from near St Mullins in south Carlow, both of whom had the word *treddles* for the marble-shaped dung of rabbits, hares and sheep. This old word is from Old English *tyrdel*, Middle English *tirdel, tridel*, a diminutive of *turd*. My Surrey friend, unaware that treddles is a dialect word and not standard, was surprised at my delight at hearing it again.

Another good word that was alive in south Carlow when I was

young was *swope*, a drink, and as a verb, to drink, to guzzle. 'He'd swope the Barrow dry.' Variants are found all over England and Scotland; and in the baronies of Forth and Bargy long ago, they had *zap*. Related to the more common *sup*, from Old English *sopa*, old Norse *sopi*, a mouthful.

A word P.J. McGowran heard near Monaghan town many years ago is *trawly*, an adjective used exclusively, he tells me, of saucy young girls. A trawly girl was, in the euphemistic speech of the more matronly females of the day, 'a girl who stayed out late at night'. This trawly comes from the Irish noun *tráill*, a slave, a wretched person. Nothing like a trawly girl to put a grush on the oul' wans of yesteryear. *Grush* is also a good Monaghan word. There it means an unpleasant face; its Irish antecedent, *gnúis*, simply means face, appearance.

## Boxing Harry – Scrocky

The Dublin taxi-driver was talking about Paul McCartney being knighted. He knew him, he said, in harder times than these, when Paul had to box Harry. Who, I politely inquired, was Harry? I could not quite envisage Sir Paul fighting his way out of the proverbial paper bag.

'Squire,' said my driver, 'you mustn't know Liverpool. I was brought up there. To box Harry meant to pull the devil by the tail, if you know what that means.'

I subsequently found the expression *to box Harry* in many of the dialect dictionaries of northern England. It means to go without food; to make do with scraps of food; to rough it; to take what comes. In *Notes and Queries* for 1883 we are told that the phrase was in vogue then among commercial travellers, implying dinner and tea at one meal.

But who was Harry? Well, Harry was the Devil, and the Liverpool phrase meant, of course, to take on the Devil. The boyo was also known in this country as Harry: you'd still hear the more genteel among the swearing classes say, 'be the Lord Harry!'

Margaret Power's mother made colcannon in the oul' skillet pot, just like the lady in the song. 'I'd like to know the origin of *skillet*', she says. 'Where my mother came from, Slieverue in south Kilkenny, Irish was spoken until the turn of the century, and I've often wondered if it's Irish.'

The Irish, *scilléad*, is a borrowing from English, but where the English came from is a bit of a mystery. Collins says that it's related to Middle English word *skele*, which in turn is from the Old Norse *skjola*, a bucket. Oxford pleads ignorance. I think skillet may have come in with Margaret's ancestors. The Old French has the word *escuelette*, *a* dish. Apart from being set before one on the table it was also used in cooking.

'You may or may not be familiar with a word which, having never seen it spelled, I'll write as *ardhews*, emphasis on the second syllable. The old people around Kingscourt used it a lot when I was growing up, and that's not today or yesterday. They'd say, "Ah sure, don't heed the poor gossons, it's only the ardhews," when they made excuses for high jinks that had got out of hand at a wake, say. Can you throw any light on this word for me?' Thus spake Mary O'Hanlon, who now lives not far from Cambridge.

The excellent *Ulster Dialect Dictionary* has this as '*ardhughs*, noun, plural, antics, capers, origin unknown'. I'd say, without fear of contradiction, that the origin is the Irish *ardú*; here it has the English -s plural ending. Ó Dónaill's dictionary defines *ardú* as excitement as well as the verbal noun of *ardaigh*, rise.

It's not unknown in the south either. An old Glenmore, Co. Kilkenny, woman to whom I mentioned in my long-lost youth that I had never seen anything in my life as sexy as La Monroe singing that song in *Some Like It Hot*, said that she might send her husband to the pictures to see if Marilyn would give him *th'ardoo* as well. The priapic slant, if that's the correct phrase in this context, would not, I feel, have been included in the *Ulster Dialect Dictionary*, where 'obscenities have been omitted where it was thought they might cause offence'. From a *dialect* dictionary, for God's sake?

Jürgen Kullmann, writing from Dortmund in a mixture of English and impeccable Irish which he learned over the years while on holiday in Connemara, asks about the word *haggard,* which, he says, is not to be found in even the best English–German dictionaries.

The reason for this is that *haggard* is regarded as a dialect word that would not be understood nowadays in many parts of rural England; it is confined to Ireland, Scotland, the Isle of Man and parts of England's West Country, according to both the EDD and the latest surveys. It is an old word; its origin is the Old Norse *heygarthr,* from *hey,* hay and *garthr,* yard.

Eleanor Annesley, who lives in Poole in Dorset, but who comes from Gloucestershire, has started reading this column thanks to some nice things William Trevor said about it. 'I was recently taken to dinner in a lovely restaurant near Truro,' she writes, 'and I was shocked to find on the menu an item described as "gobbets of venison marinated in red wine". Now, I've always known a *gobbet* as a lump of sputum, and I was a little put off by the Cornish word, which is in common use.'

Yes, sputum is what comes to my mind too, when I hear of gobbets, Eleanor, but I've heard *gobbets,* morsels of food, used in your own lovely Dorset as well as in Devon and Cornwall. The word is common in this sense in Scotland as well. Scott, in *Redgauntlet,* has 'He immediately began to transfer the mutton and pie crust from the plate to his lips in such huge gobbets, as if he was refreshing a threedays fast.' Tindale used the word in 1526 in rendering Matthew: 'And they gadered vp of the gobbetys that remained xij full.'

Earlier, (1388) Wyclif had *gobetys.* So, *gobbets* has a more illustrious pedigree than the 20th-century import *medallions* or, as they say in the more pretentious places, 'Medaillons, monsewer'.

As to where the word came from, Dumeril is sure that it came from the Norman French *gobet,* a morsel, from *gober,* to gulp down. Fair enough, but an Irishman might ask if the French word, and the English *gob,* a mouth, found in a hundred compounds such as *gobsmacked* and *gobshite*, are connected with Irish *gob*, *gop*, a beak, snout, muzzle, used here in beautiful nature poems when Christianity was young. Perhaps. I'd be reluctant to go further than that.


# Caff


I was much taken by a word used by a northern friend of mine when he was holding forth on the merits, such as they are, of our present rugby squad. 'Too much *caff* in there to beat Scotland,' he predicted gloomily. *Caff* is a variant of *chaff*. Perhaps I should say that *chaff* is a variant of *caff* which is now relegated to dialect status, I'm afraid. Its origin is the Old English *caff*, in places, *ceaf*. The word was spelled *caife* in 1330 in Hampole's Psalms: 'We sall drife thaim fra vs, as caif fra corne.' Burns, whom I've been re-reading lately, had 'The cleanest corn that e'er was dight, May hae some pyles o'caff in' in his *Address to the Unco Guid*. My northern friend was using the word in a figurative sense. Any useless or worthless thing could be called *caff*, even if the object in question was a forward about the size of a small steamroller.

*Caff* is found in Scotland and in the north of England as well. In Yorkshire they have the adjective *caffy*, useless, mean. In Cornwall *caff* is refuse, rubbish of any kind, particularly unsaleable fish.

There are some interesting compounds. A *caff-bed* was a bed-tick filled with chaff instead of feathers, and *caff-riddling* was a St Mark's Eve custom I wouldn't like to have anything to do with. This old explanation from Yorkshire will tell you why: 'The riddle is filled with chaff, the scene of operations being the barn floor, with both barn doors being set wide open: the hour is midnight or just before, and each person of the party takes the riddle in succession and riddles the contents. The appearance of a funeral procession, or of persons bearing a coffin, is a certain augury of death, either to the then riddler himself or someone near to him.'

In parts of west Co. Waterford, they have another *caff*, a verb which means to irritate a person by making fun of him. The late Dr Risteard Breatnach of Slieverue and UCD gave me the word.

This *caff* is from the Old French *calfer*, *caufer*, whence the modern *chauffer*, to warm, heat.

## Boak – Coppulhurish – Capall

Ian Shuttleworth of Bunbury Avenue, Belfast, had heard the verb *to boak* only in his home area of north Lincolnshire until he came across it in east Belfast. It means, to retch, vomit; to belch. Mr Shuttleworth wonders which way did the tide flow: did *boak* reach Belfast from across the water, or did Ulster people bring it with them to the towns and fields of places like Lincolnshire?

*Boak* is found in many places under many guises, *bock*, *balk*, *bouch*, *bouk*, *bowk*, *boac* among them. The word has been located all over Britain, from Scotland to Kent and Pembrokeshire. The word was regarded as very coarse in England, but the earthy Scots had no trouble with it. In 1807, that down-to-earth observer of Scottish social customs, Beatties, tells us about a genteel Aberdeen party at which 'some were boukin ahint the door'.

The word is still common in Donegal. From Middle English *bolken*, *bulken*, to belch, throw up, from Old English *bealcan*, same meaning.

Tom Smith from Rathfarnham was born near Carrick, Co. Monaghan, four score years ago. A word of his youth is *coppulhurish*. It means a see-saw. He wonders where it came from.

Well, some say that it is from the Irish *capall thairis*, 'horse over, or across, it.' Dinneen has *capall corrach*, a term used by a Rosses woman, Mary Sweeney from Meenbanad, in the late 1950s. She sat at her window watching a few kids setting one up in her street. She hadn't seen a capall corrach since she was a wee wain, she said, a long time ago, aye. She was approaching 104 at the time. *Corrach* in this phrase means uneven, unstable. Perhaps *thairis* was transmuted into *corrach*. Stranger things have happened to words.

An interesting word this *capall* of ours. In Ulster Irish and in Scots Gaelic it means a mare rather than a horse, entire or cut. The word does not correspond to the Latin *caballus*, according to the scholars: they point to a modified form such as *cappillus*.

*Caple, capul, capyle* and *capo* are found in Scots and in the English of Chester and Lancashire. Shadwell in *The Lancashire Witches*, a play of 1692, has 'I am turned into a horse, a capo, a meer titt.' Chaucer wrote of 'bothe hey and cart, and eek hise caples three' in the *Canterbury Tales*. We find 'Conscience on his capul' in *Piers Plowman*. The Icelandic is *kappul*. All from that mysterious *cappillus*, I suspect, rather, than borrowed from our old word for a work-horse.

## Ray — Scrud — Skrau

A man who lives in Balbriggan has sent me three interesting words. He is well aware of the many old dialect words that still survive in Fingall, especially among the older people. His first word he spells *ray*. The sentence he gave as a help to me is: 'The cow is over in the ray.' Ah, I said to myself, simplicity itself. The same word as the great Clare hurler of my day, Jimmy Smyth, gave me, a flat field; a flat upland moor. The Irish *ré*, of course. I phoned my Balbriggan friend to ask would this meaning fit his *ray*. Not a bit of it. His word meant the corner of a field. I went searching again and found his *ray* for him in Scandinavia. The Old Norse is *vra*, a corner, a nook.

His second word is *scrud*. His sentence: 'She had no more than a scrud of a dress on her.' He heard this from his late mother, who was born in 1890. He insists the word is not *screed*, a shred of clothing. The word is not in any of the great dictionaries, All I can offer is that it may well be a variant of *screed*, which comes from the Old English *screade*, influenced by Scandinavian words beginning with *sk*, the American World Books Dictionary tells me. So back I went to Scandinavia and among the *sk* words I found *skrud*, Old Icelandic, Swedish, dress, attire. Anois tú!

The third word was *skrau*, to scrape, scratch. Also a noun. This word, still common in the English of Tipperary, is easily identified as Irish *scrabhadh*, noun and verb. I can trace the Irish word no further back than the beginning of the 18th century, when the poet Aodhagán Ó Rathaille used it, but I now find that *skrau*, in various other spellings, is common all over England. The EDD has 'I scrowed all the skin off my arm.' In the Lake District a scrow is a mark cut in the bark of trees destined to be felled.

Its origin? It's from Middle English *scrowle*, alteration, after *rowle* (still a common Irish pronunciation of *roll*), of *scrow*, aphetic or foreshortened form of Anglo-Norman *escrowe*, a strip of parchment. Thus it's related to *scroll*. From the parchment to the scrawb made on it by penmen is not such a leap, is it?

## Tallamacka – Oxer – Spen

Mainchín Seoighe from Tankardstown, Kilmallock, wrote to tell me that one of his mother's words for clamour, noisy disagreement, hullaballoo, was *tallamacka*. The good lady was from Bruree, a fair old step from Tullogher, Co. Kilkenny, where Séamus Moylan found *telemachus*, a word with the same meaning. John Rochford, writing from Waterford city, tells me that he has heard *tallymackey* in the footholds of the Comeragh mountains. A mysterious word in all its variants. And I still have no notion where it originated.

R. Burke of Galway wrote to ask about a term used in commentaries on showjumping: an *oxer*. The old regional dialect dictionaries of England give the word as foxhunting slang for a tall, dense fence, capable of withstanding the efforts of an ox to escape; an ox-fence. In 1861 a foxhunting man wrote: 'The fence was an oxer, about seven feet high and impervious to a bird.' Interestingly, the EDD says that an oxer is 'a post and a single rail alongside a fence to keep cattle off the fence.' The word seems to be no older than the mid-19th century. Still used in Leicestershire among hunting people, I'm told; in showjumping slang since about 1930.

A shy farmer from the foot of Mount Leinster asks if I've ever come across the word *spen*. It means the teat of an animal, especially that of a cow.

*Spen*, also found as *spin*, *spean* and *speen*, seems to be confined nowadays mainly to the south of England and Wales. Pembrokeshire has *spen*, and as *spen* Jacob Poole, the Quaker farmer and amateur word-man, found it in south-east Wexford at the end of the 18th century. The word is from the Old Norse *speni*, a teat.

There is another *spean*, but rare in Ireland, my spies in Macra na Feirme inform me. This word was sent to me by a lady from Kilmacthomas in Co. Waterford. Her father's word, it means the prong of a hay or dung-fork. My friend hasn't heard it in years. Found also in southern England, nobody seems to know its origin. Latin *spina*, a thorn?

Still another *spen/spean/speen/spain/spene* meaning to wean, is found all over England's north country, Scotland and Ulster. 'But wither'd beldams, loud an'droll, Rigwooddie hags would spean a foal' wrote the great Ayrshireman in *Tam o' Shanter*. In Ulster a spen is a child recently separated from its mother's breast, and so inclined to be a little cross. Of Teutonic origin. Compare Middle Dutch and Middle Low German *spanen*, *spenen*.


## Alibi – Umpire – Shire – County – Rape

An English soccer manager, interviewed on television recently after his team's poor performance, said that he had no alibi. I'm sure he meant excuse; at all events, M.F. Gibson of Clontarf wants to know where *alibi* came from. The word *umpire* also bothers him.

Alibi is the Latin *alibi*, elsewhere, from *alius*, other, plus *bi* as in *ubi*, where. Hence the sense extension 'somewhere else' – evidence introduced in court to show that the accused couldn't have done it, your Honour, because he was somewhere else at the time.

*Excuse* is from Latin, *excusare*, itself from *ex*, outside of, plus *cusare*, from *causa*, accusation. Perhaps the soccer manager had no excuses to offer, but Mr Gibson surely deserved an *explanation*, a word in English law books since the 15th century. Explain is from Latin *explanare*. The *planare* bit means to flatten, from *planus*, level.

Umpire is trickier. The word comes by mistaken division from a *noumpere*, from Old French *nomper*, not one of a pair. Nomper is made of *nom*, *non*, not, and *per*, equal, a relative of peer. Originally the ref in duelling.

Martin Holden a Kilkenny man living in Sussex, was giving his thoughts lately to shires and counties. He wonders why we don't have shires in Ireland. We don't have them because we didn't have a Saxon dynasty here. Shire is from Old English *scir*, office, from Old High German *scira*, business. This strip of land, this *shire*, was governed by an earl in the king's name in Saxon England.

After the Norman invasion the earl was replaced by a count, a title borrowed from the later Roman empire. Originally it meant companion – Latin *comes*. The earl's shire was now the count's county – Latin *comitatus*. But as happens in the strange and often inexplicable fortune of words, the count has disappeared from the titles of the English nobility, while the earl has recovered his position; and the countess is now the wife of an earl.

Martin lives in the Rape of Bramber, he tells me. He knows that *rape* was a Saxon division of some sort, just as our baronies were. Yes, there were Saxon *hundreds*, a group or settlement of one hundred free families of Saxon incomers, and Saxon rapes, districts in which twenty or more peasants maintained one poor person. The word, and the remarkable charity, are Scandinavian in origin. The Old Icelandic was *hreppr*.

## Busk and Busking

Could you tell me where the word *busk* comes from, writes Mary White from Raheny, to which I must reply, which *busk*, Mary?

If you mean the verb to play music in the streets for money, to busk may be from the Italian *buscare*, a word John Florio, lexicographer and adviser on cultural, and possibly other matters, to James the First's queen, Anne of Denmark, has in his great dictionary. To him it meant 'to prowle, to filch, to shift for'. Then again it may be from the Spanish *buscar*, to seek, from Old Spanish *boscar*, perhaps originally to hunt by beating a wood (*bosco*). This is Oxford's guess. Another cognate word is the old French *busquer*, 'to shift, prowle', according to the 17th-century Cotgrave, who had read Florio.

What in God's name has this to do with playing music on the streets?

Well, as late as the 19th century to *busk* meant to get money by any means which would prevent a policeman from saying you were begging. You could busk, or be a busker, by singing or dancing or playing music, by selling matches or flowers, or by cutting silhouettes in pubs, a favourite form of busking according to Mayhew in 1851. Collins says that busk, to play music, is a 20th-century word. Really?

The late Mike Flynn of Kilmore, Co. Wexford told me once that a *busker* was a fisherman who went to sea in all weathers. Mike's mother used to make *busks* for them at Shrovetide. These were buns made from white flour, cinnamon and sugar.

Another Wexford *busk* would be known in other airts as a *bodhrán*, traditional tambourine.

Phil Wall of Carne, who was 90 when I met him in the late sixties, called a milksop a *busker*. Interestingly, in Devon and Dorset a *busker* is, or was, a calf left too long unweaned.

Then there is *busk*, a bush in Norfolk, a bunch of flowers in west Waterford. Old Norse *buskr*.

*To busk* in Ayrshire still means to dress, deck out, adorn. 'A bonny bride is soon busked.' This is from Old Norse *buask*, to make oneself ready, from *bua*, to prepare.

Finally *busk*, a stiffener in an old-fashioned corset, is from Old Italian *busco*, a splinter, a stick. In Cornwall, I'm reliably informed, it means something else as well. You can guess what, Mary White. I'm not going to be the one to corrupt you.

## Blather – Bars – Joolee

The word *blather*, foolish talk, or as my correspondent, Mary Regan from Cork, has it, 'oul guff', is found all over this island. Is it Irish? the good lady asks.

Well, it certainly is in Irish as *bladar*. The Kerry poet, Eoghan Rua Ó Súilleabháin, lamented the fact that he spent so much time 'ag bladar le béithibh' – blathering with beauties, in the hope of showing them his etchings or whatever; but *blather*, and its variants *bledder*, *blether*, etc., are found all over Britain, from Scotland to Somerset. Hence we get *blathering*, *bletherin'*, etc. 'Thou ne'er took such a bleth'ran bitch into thy dark dominion,' wrote Rab Burns in a cross mood.

To blather, etc., also meant to make a disturbance or commotion, to cry out. Grose (1790) tells us that in the north-east of Ireland to blather was 'to make a loud clattering noise by striking with sticks, cabbage stocks, etc., against people's doors after dark and then running off. This custom, though fast wearing out, is still practised by boys on the Eve of All Hallows.'

Anyway, *blather* came our way courtesy of our Norse friends. *Blathra* meant to talk nonsense. The word also survives to this day in Swedish dialect *bladdra* and in Norwegian dialect *bledra*.

'Have you any big *bars* at all?,' the lady in Charlie Hamilton's of Newtownstewart asked me. What's left of my mind tossed this one around, and the penny dropped. Máire Nic Mhaoláin had sent me this word, I remembered. She had heard it in Derry. Its origin is in the Irish phrase *barr nuachta*. Dinneen has 'An bhfuil aon bharr nuaidheachta agat?' from Aran. He explained it as 'have you any strange news?' 'Ach, we don't speak Irish around here,' said the nice young girl in the shop. That's true, God knows, but neither do they speak Norse in Newtownstewart, where *blather* survives.

A friend reminded me recently of the rather strange pronunciation some of the old people who lived in the beautiful valleys between Céim an Fhia and Bantry had for the month of July. The closest I can get to it is *Joolee*; emphasis on the first syllable, and with the broad Irish 'l'. We may have laughed long ago in our ignorance, but this pronunciation is a survival from the 17th century. It was still common in 1798 when Wordsworth rhymed July with truly: 'In March, December and in July ... The neighbours tell, and tell you truly ...' That's what my friend Jer Glas would have written, had the Muse so ordained.

## Beknowst – Smithereens – Bobbery – Speer Wall

I continue to be surprised by the number of words thought to belong only to the English of Ireland that crop up in the dialects of England.

Take the verb *to beknow*, meaning to know, understand, acknowledge. Many's the time I've heard it in south Carlow, most recently at the funeral of a young man drowned in the Barrow. A woman said to another: 'Isn't it terrible to think he didn't beknow how dangerous that place is.' You'll hear *beknow*, meaning acknowledge, too; *beknownst* as well, and *unbeknownst*, and more than once I've seen it written that the words are exclusively Anglo-Irish. Nonsense. They are found too in Essex and Somerset, according to Joseph Wright's great dictionary. In *Piers Plowman* (*c.*1362) you'll find 'Ichau ben covetous, quod this caityf (prisoner) I beknowe (acknowledge) hit here'; and Chaucer, in the *Canterbury Tales* (late 1300s) wrote: 'I dar noght biknowe myn owne name.'

Yes, it's dangerous to assume that a word is native to any particular place. The OED, sensibly, has *smithereens* as being 'adopted from, or the source of Irish *smidirín*; their doubt is caused by the existence of the English dialect *smithers*, fragments, a word known to Dickens. And I was very surprised indeed to find that the Oirish exclamation *bejapers!*, so beloved of English comedians, is far more commonly used in Yorkshire and in East Anglia than it is in Ireland.

Mr J. Lundon, a Limerickman now living in Knockaunglass, Athenry, has in his time sent me very interesting words, exclusive of those he uses to denigrate Wexford hurling. He has recently sent me a word still heard in mid-Tipperary and east Limerick: *bobbery*, a slang word meaning noise, noisy disturbance, row. He informs me that it is an Anglo-Indian representation of Hindi *Bap re!* O father! – a common expression of surprise or grief. It seems to have first found its way into print in 1816 in a tome called *Adventures in Hindostan*. When it arrived in Limerick and Tipp is anybody's guess.

Finally, Mary White from Wexford asks where the expression *speer wall*, a partition near the door of a farmhouse, originated. The speer wall didn't run the length of the kitchen, just far enough to prevent a draught between the farmhouse door and the open fire. I have myself heard this word in Kilmore Quay. A lovely survival this, ultimately, I think, from the Old English *gespearrian*, to shut, bar. Is it found elsewhere in Ireland?

## The Real Alie Daley – Clamper – Birse

Patricia McCormack recently asked about the origins of the phrase *the real Alie Daly*. I've had a fascinating letter about the matter, pointing to a Limerick lady who lived when Dan O'Connell was dragging us off our knees.

Thanks to Bernadette Lee from Saxville, New York, home on holidays in her relations' house in Beechpark Road, Foxrock, Dublin. She wrote: 'As regards Alie Daly, I believe I have the answer. Alice Daly, my great-greatgrandmother, was married to Patrick Lee of Ballintubber, Co. Limerick. She was known for the fine quality of her buttermaking, and she sold her product at the market in Mitchelstown. My brother, Michael Lee of Thurles, the family historian, estimates the date of her birth at around 1800. I've been told that the test for estimating the quality of butter being sold at the market was done in those days by drawing a finger across the firkin, and then tasting it. When Alice's butter was tasted one day, somebody said, "That's the real Alie Daly". The phrase survived. '

*Clamper* is a word used in the eastern part of Galway, so writes J.S. of Tuam, who wants to know the origin of the word, which means wrangling, disputation, trouble. 'There's going to be one almighty clamper when she finds out he brought the other one home from the dance,' is my friend's example of the use of the word. This is the Irish *clampar*, commotion, trouble.

The anonymous play, *Captain Thomas Stukeley*, written around 1600, has: 'Esta clamper, thoo talkest too much.' (Éist do chlampar: silence your noise.) The rather more coarse *The Irish Hudibras* (1689) has 'Let not dy ars make a Clamp-peer, Lest vid a Fart dou blow it from me.'

I haven't been able to trace the Irish *clampar* further back than 1583, and I think Irish borrowed it from English. You see, there is the English dialect word *clamper*, which means 1. To make a clattering noise; 2. A difficulty; something troublesome. This clamper is from Low German *klampern*, to make a noise.

Mary Smith from Monaghan asks where her mother's word *birse*, meaning anger, came from. 'Don't rise me birse,' the good woman would warn before she'd start a clamper. This is a figurative use of *birse*, a word still common in Scotland. It comes from Old English *byrst*, a bristle.

## Cranking – Slocken – Latching on

If you listen carefully in fishing towns and villages you are likely to hear interesting usages that are not agree to this country, as they say in Kilmore Quay; that is, not natives of Ireland (*agree* is from Old French *agreer*). I heard the word *cranking* used in Dungarvan recently by an oldtimer who came from Helvick direction. He was referring to a gentleman who was murdering James Connolly, the Irish rebelle, in the corner of the hotel lounge, to the detriment of civilised conversation, and my new-found friend muttered something about a crankin' gommul.

Wright has *crank* in the Helvickman's sense in the EDD: 'to sing dolefully, to croak'. John Clare, in *The Shepherd's Calendar*, wrote a 'a solitary crane ... Cranking a jarring melancholy strain'. I have never come across a mention of Ireland in relation to this type of cranking, so how did the word come to west Waterford? An entry in *Swainson's Birds* of 1885 may point to the answer: 'The lesser spotted woodpecker is sometimes called the Crank-bird from the cry of the bird resembling the creaking produced by the turning of a windlass.' So we may look to the sea.

Brigid O'Donnell of Red Ard, Culdaff, Co. Donegal, has sent me a valuable list of words, many of them unknown to me. One of them she spells *slócan,* and *to slócan*, she explains, means 'to add solids to minimise the amount of liquid'.

I must confess to being puzzled by this one. I don't think it could be related to *slocken*, sometimes spelled *slockan* in Ulster literature, a verb meaning to slake, to cool with water; to drench, quench, extinguish. *To slockan* also means to choke with mud or water. Not Brigid's word, I think, but a fine Scots and Ulster word in its own right.

Burns has 'I've even joined the honoured jorum, When mighty

Squireships of the quorum. Their hydra drout did sloken.' The
*Ballymena Observer* of 1882 (a book, by the way, not a newspaper)
has 'That's a very slokenin' drink.' The EDD has this from Lincolnshire: 'The land is that slackened wi' watter it'll take a munth
o' dry weather to reightle it.' This *slocken* is from the Old Norse
*slokna*, to be extinguished.

The phrase '*to latch on to*' something troubles Jack Barry from
Sunday's Well in Cork. Modern slang? he asks. Far from it. You'll
find this latch in the York Plays of about 1400; it comes from the
Anglo Saxon *laeccan*, to catch, seize.


## William Carleton and Lady Morgan

One of the more farcical aspect of Irish literature in the 19th century was the attempt by the writers to compose spellings that, they
hoped, would approximate to the sounds of original Irish words
still in use in the newly-learned English of the period. Careleton
made an unholy botch of things. *Vich na hoiah* was his rendering of
*a mhic na hoighe*, son of the Virgin. Michael Banim, a native speaker,
one supposes, from Kilkenny, talks of *arguff chase* when he meant
*airgead síos*, money down, and he made *nor-i-een-thoo-lath* out of *an
airionn tú leat* (mé), do you hear me.

Lady Morgan, born 1783, she of *The Wild Irish Girl* fame, was
the best of them in this regard. She has the occasional howler, but
she often left the Irish English words in their original spelling, and
when she didn't, she deserves a pass, if not an honour, in her
attempts to convey the sound of the original words. Interesting
words many of the are. Writing of fresh milk, she has: 'To supply
the want of this, by them highly esteemed luxury, they cut an
onion into a bowl of water, into which they dip their potatoes.
This they call a *scadan caoch*, or blind herring.' This phrase, written
as *scaddan keek*, was recently sent to me by a Naas woman, who
glossed it as 'A poor substitute for something. You might say that
compared to the potato dug from the earth, instant mash is only a
scaddan keek.'

Lady Morgan's *binnogue* is still in use. This, she tells us, 'is a handkerchief lightly folded around the brows, and curiously fastened under the chin'. The late Dr Richard Walsh recorded this word in south Kilkenny. It was, he told me, a handkerchief worn by women milking cows or baking bread. Irish *binneog*.

*Troithíní* was another of Lady Morgan's words, but she spelled the word *triathians*. 'A pair of yarn nose which scarcely reached mid-leg, and left ankle and foot naked,' she tells us. The word *troithín* is still in use. 'An old brogue will get an old troithín any day' was a phrase jotted down in Westmeath by the scholar, Eamonn Mac an Fhailigh, in our own time. The allusion is to amorous old couples, I need hardly say.

## Frowsy – Guff – Tocher – Salad Days

I heard the word *frowsy* used recently by a man who was born and reared in Co. Antrim. It is in Patterson's Glossary of Antrim words, a work older than the century, and it means musty, ill-smelling, fetid. The word is also applied to untidy, matted hair, and Patterson gives us 'Your hair looks very frowzy.' In England a frowsy person is bad-tempered, peevish; and the word is used of anything disordered and offensive to the eye or nose.

The Americans have a variant, *frowy*, which I've heard applied to bread as it becomes stale, and to milk going sour. This is an Elizabethan word. Spenser has 'They soone myght ... like not of the frowie fede' in the *Shepherd's Calendar*.

My Antrim friend also used the word *guff*, a word common all over Ireland and Scotland, but very rare indeed, I'm told, in England. It means, of course, babble, foolish talk. Where it comes from is another matter. I think it is of Scandinavian origin; we may compare the Norwegian dialect *gufs*, a puff of wind and the older *guffs*, to blow softly.

From Bangor J.S. Hogg writes to inquire about a word used by some of the older people in the Ards peninsula: *tocher*, a woman's dowry. The word has died out, Mr Hogg tells me, because the dowry is a thing of the past.

An import from Scotland, this. Ramsay's *Proverbs* (1737), a book I'd love to see republished, has 'Better a tocher in her than wi' her.' Burns has the compound *tocher-band* in *The Gallant Weaver*: 'My daddie sign'd my *tocher-band*.' He meant the articles for the disposal of the woman's dowry.

The word is from Scots Gaelic, *tochar*, dowry.

Finally, Mary Walker, a young lady from Dalkey who has just done her Leaving Certificate, wrote to ask about the origin of the phrase, *salad days*, that lovely time of youth and inexperience. Shakespeare coined it, in *Antony and Cleopatra*: 'My salad days, When I was green in judgement, cold in blood.' Enjoy the holidays, Mary, and if you are tired of the books, remember Thomas Hood's quatrain written when he too was exhausted from mental strain: 'My temples throb, my pulses boil, I'm tired of song and ode and ballad; Come, Thyrsis, get the midnight oil, And pour it on a lobster salad.'

## Some Horsey Words

'You seem to know a bit about horses, unlike your fellow Yellowbelly, John Banville, who told us last year that he had discovered the lovely word *surcingle* and was waiting for a chance to use it,' wrote Flor Crowley, who forgot to put his address on his letter, which has a Bandon postmark. 'Anyway, could you tell me anything about a word I've heard horse-traders use over the years? You often find an ill-used horse whose hair, just below the withers or on his back, has turned white from the rubbing of a badly-fitting saddle. The phrase I've heard is 'That's bad peel'. Is this the same peel as in 'to peel an orange' or is there a more interesting history?"

*Peel* in orange-peel is from Old English *pilian,* to strip off the outer layer. The horse-copers' *peel* is from French, *peler* used in ancient times to mean to lose hair, to fleece. Both *pilian* and *peler* are from the Latin *pilare,* to make bald, from *pilus,* a hair.

I'm not with you about John Banville's *surcingle,* a beautiful word, I agree, meaning a girth for a horse to keep the saddle in place. The word is from Old French *surcengle*, from *sur*, over and *cengle*, a belt, from Latin *cingulum*. The Irish is the even lovelier-sounding *sursaing*.

Speaking of horses, my tentative incursions into the speech of the travelling people brought to light that the word they so rightly hate, *knacker*, was to them, in days gone by, an honourable and proud appellation.

In the 19th century the word was usually spelled *nacker,* and a nacker was a saddler, or harness-maker. Collins now gives *(k)nacker* as 'Irish slang, a despicable person'; but I know old Wexford farmers who told me that in their fathers' time the nacker, the travelling harness-maker, was a very welcome guest indeed. He saved the expense of a long journey to town to have surcingles, bridles and saddles mended by some brogue-maker who wouldn't know a peel from a bog-spavin.

An old word, this nacker, as may be seen from its ancestors,. the 16th-century English *nacker*, saddler, and the Old Norse *knakkur*, a saddle.

The same Old Norse word is the ancestor of knacker, a person who buys horses for slaughter, and, Collins assures me, also a person who buys old houses with the purpose of demolishing them, selling their interiors for scrap, and building new houses in their place. Isn't there a more genteel word for that knacker? A developer, isn't it?

## *Holyawn — Leeawn — Shebinock — Sheelafeeka*

Margaret Whitty from Wexford asks about a word common enough in that county, but not so common elsewhere, I suspect –*holyawn*. That's how Margaret spells it, and that's how Patrick Kennedy spelled it a century and a half ago in *A View from Mount Leinster,* where a put-upon crathur thanked God 'for having no young holyawns to trouble me any more'. I heard the word in the south east of the county from the late Liz Jeffries of Kilmore, who described a four-year-old who amused himself throwing stones at her front door, as 'the greatest little holyawn in the parish'. As to the word's origin, I suspect it was once the Irish *teolán*, a little thief. Dinneen has *teol*, theft without concealment, and hence *teolaí*, a thief.

Please tell me something about the word *leeawn*, pleads an anonymous person who wrote from Leinster House. 'I've heard the word used of women who are thrushtin' 60, and that in my part of the country means that they are just about past getting a man,' writes my correspondent, who, I would guess, is of the male persuasion.

The word as Dinneen has it is *laoidhean*, the portion of a potato left after 'eyes' are cut for sowing. There are many words for this, the discarded part of a seed spud. One that comes to mind is *clofferteen*, derived from Irish *clafairtín*, I'm assured. I can't find this one in the dictionaries, but Fr Michael Comer has it in an article he wrote in *Beacán/Beken. A Portrait of an East Mayo Parish*, in the not too distant past.

'How would you like a tare out of that shebinock?', was an expression I overheard in a hotel lounge in Macroom. The question was put by a lady of a certain vintage to an equally mature woman, two friends who had come from the hinterland to buy the Christmas, as they say in their part of the country. They were having a drop of port, while appearing to enjoy the spectacle of two Sumo wrestlers in action on the television. *Shebinock* is the Irish *seibineach*, and it is quite common in rural Ireland. In west Cork it means a big fat cat. In Tipperary it is a big rabbit, or rat. In Mayo it is a big strong man; in Clare, a woman of imposing stature.

The word is not one of disparagement. *Sheelafeeka*, a word sent to me by a shy lady from Thurles, is. She recently heard it applied to a television soccer pundit. It is the Irish *Síle a' Phíce*, one of the ninety-six words we have for an earwig.

## Skidaddle

*Skidaddle*, often spelled *skedaddle*, is a word that has been bothering Jack Morrison of Sandymount, Dublin, late of New York, as the country hairdressers used to say in their advertisements. The word's history is what intrigues Mr M. He has consulted the dictionaries and has found no joy.

All of them say that the word is of unknown origin and not older than the 19th century. 'Come on, now,' exhorts Jack, 'you wrote once that when in doubt look at the dialects. Any ideas?'

Well now, I see that the 1864 edition of Webster, the great American dictionary, has: 'Said to be of Swedish or Danish origin, and to have been in common use for several years throughout the Northwest in the vicinity of immigrants from those nations.'

But Oxford doesn't agree, as there are no forms in Swedish or Danish sufficiently near to be seriously taken into account. Oxford says that 'there is some slight evidence of the currency of the word before it became prominent in America, but it is doubtful how far this is important for its origin.'

This 'slight evidence', I think, is the English dialect and Scots word *skedaddle*, 'applied to the wasteful over-flow of the milk in pails, when the milkmaids do not balance them properly', according to the 19th-century Scots word-man, Mackay; and not long after the American Civil War, the *Atlantic Journal* has a correspondent from Lancashire giving out about what he considered the American misuse of the word: 'We heard *skedaddle* every day of our lives. It means to scatter, or drop in a scattering way. If you run with a bucket of potatoes or apples, and keep spilling some of them, in an irregular way along the path, you are said to skedaddle them.'

The word came into US military slang during the Civil War. The *New York Tribune* of 10 August 1861 has: 'No sooner did the traitors discover their approach than they skedaddled (a phrase the Union boys here apply to the good use the 'seceshers' make of their legs in time of danger).'

But, to Mr Morrison's question. I have convinced myself that the word is not a fanciful formation, as Oxford has decided, but an inspired fusion of two old dialect words. The first is *skid*, to slip away. The second is another English North Country and Scottish word, *scaddle*, as old as the 15th century. It means to run off in fright. American papers please copy. Oxford and Collins too, if you are interested.

# Douce — Ramsack — Fardel

Ann Kennedy of Belfast wrote about her mother's word *douce,* meaning well-to-do.

Douce means a variety of things. Pronounced *doose,* by the way, as an adjective it means gentle, kind, pleasant, cheerful, hospitable. The word is also used as an adverb. Watt, in his *Poetic Sketches* of 1880, has: 'The rude norlin' blast ... Was douce as the westlin' breeze.' The same man has *doucely* as an adverb: 'Hoo doucely she looks in her auld hamely claes.' Douce also means sedate, respectable. There is a Scots proverb, 'Wanton kittens make douce cats.' Hamilton, in his *Poems* of 1865, speaks a young lady who was, in Seán Ó Faoláin's phrase, a little weak in the carnalities: 'Puir May was packit frae the hoose By Rabbie's mither snell an' douce.' *Snell* means severe.

In the north of Ireland douce means, tidy, neat, comfortable, applied to both persons and things. The *Ballymena Observer* (1892) said that word was then applied to elderly housewives. Simmons in his Donegal *Glossary* of 1890 glosses douce as 'thriving, prosperous'.

I've never heard douce in the south. As to its origin, it comes from the French *douce* sweet, pleasant.

An interesting letter from Mary Gladney, a Carlow woman. 'When I was young,' she writes, 'the universal pronunciation of *ransack* was *ramsack*. I speak of the south of the county, along the border with Kilkenny and Wexford. Have you any idea why this was?'

Well, now, *ransack* comes from Old Norse *rann*, house, and *saka*, to search. The Old Norse also gave us the English *ramshackle*, a Tudor variant of the obsolete *ransackle*; a building could thus be described after the Vikings had paid it a visit. I conclude that the people who lived at the western end of the Blackstairs adopted the Tudor solecism *ram* in the first element of *ramshackle*, in their *ramsack*. I like it. Shakespeare wouldn't have lifted an eyebrow.

# Canted — Greeshkeen — Umper — Lafresh

Tom McElligott, who lives in Sutton, Co. Dublin, educator and a handballer of high renown in his day, tells me that a ball struck in error out of the court was known in the Cork of his youth as a *banished* ball. It wasn't until he came to play in Ballyanne, just outside New Ross, against the great Lyngs, Murphys and Delaneys, did he hear the term *canted* being used instead of 'banished'. A spate of letters about this cant.

It was originally the Latin *canthus*, an iron tyre. No doubt the odd Roman, forgetting his MOT test, would find his canthus flying off the wheel-rim of his chariot, causing mayhem among those walking on the roadside. Anyway, hence, eventually, the English *cant*, to bevel, slant, tilt, toss, and the new noun, fling, toss.

A lady from Athy asks where the word *greeshkeen* comes from. To her it means a loin of pork. I have found this word in various places, variously as *gríscín, grishkin, grisken, griskeen, greesteen*.

Eamon Mac an Fhailigh recorded *gríscín*, 'pork steak from an unsalted flitch', in Westmeath. I have seen it written that the word is related to the Irish *gríos*, alternative form *grís*, hot embers. Not a bit of it. It comes, I feel pretty sure, from the Old Norse *griss*, a pig, found in the modern English dialects as *grice*; and the word *griskin* has been recorded in many of the dialects of England from Northampton to Surrey. It means the lean part of a loin of pork. 'We be gwyne to kill a pig a Vriday, and we shall hay zum grisken vor dinner Zunday,' was recorded in the Isle of Wight.

John Banim, in *Crohoor of the Billhook*, written 150 years ago, has a word from Irish that still survives in Co. Laois. The word is *umper*. Banim has: 'fen tis so very asy to get an umperin all de way home for nothing.' Mary O'Reilly has heard 'Any chance of an umper?' Umper is Irish *iompar*, transport, a lift.

I have to thank Criostóir Gallagher from New Inn, Co. Tipperary, for *lafresh*, 'a drag to one side on a dress. A streel of a woman would have a lafresh on her dress'. The word, he says, seems to be confined to the Galtee region. I am delighted to have it. From Irish, *leathbhreis*, my correspondent says, a word that has, I think, escaped the nets of the lexicographers.


## *Blahs — Blackman — Blackleg — Blackfoot*

I am glad to hear that *blahs* are still made and eaten in Waterford city, and the sight of proud Waterford men and women extolling their delicacy to RTÉ's Clare McKeon on *Moveable Feast* recently reminded me of those days when my own town boasted four small bakeries whose blahs were delicious.

Clare swallowed the Waterford line about blahs being exclusive to Waterford. They may be nowadays, but, as I say, they was once made in Ross and in some of the towns of Kilkenny.

Where did it originate, this soft, spongy, delicious little flat cake of bread? France, said a Waterfordman to Clare, trying to put an exotic coating on it. A traditional Irish delicacy, I'd say, the word *blah* coming from the Irish *bleathach*. Ó Donaill's dictionary glosses this as an oatmeal cake.

'I don't recollect you ever being in need of a blackman in your young days acting the maggot around Ross,' writes a lady from my home town who signed her letter 'Guess Who?' She went on to say that she will leave a drop of whiskey for me in Jimmy Hanrahan's if I can tell the nation what a *blackman* meant in our part of the world in days gone by. 'I bet you have no idea,' she says.

Indeed I have, and I'm glad to tell my friend, whoever she is, that the word is still remembered, if not still used, between Clonroche and Enniscorthy. It meant a go-between in matters amorous; a fellow who'd introduce you to a girl, and assure her, like, that you were fairly harmless, before you got around to asking her the serious question of how her granny was for slack.

Patrick Kennedy had it in *Evenings in the Duffrey* a century and more ago: 'Started Mick on a courting expedition, giving him for a blackman a lively fidget of a farmer.'

In Scotland one of their words for a go-between is a *blackleg*. In Ulster the term is, or was, *blackfoot*. Carleton has this in *Fardorougha the Miser*: 'You want to make me a go-between, a blackfoot.'

Why *black* man, leg or foot? Now I'd buy anybody who could tell me that a Christmas drink.


## Fordel – Gool


The word *fordel* is common enough in the literature of Scotland. It means, first of all, progress, advancement. 'He has made little or no fordel', complained Sir Walter Scott of James Hogg, a master of the Scots language who spent most of the day sleeping before the huge fire of the Abbotsford kitchen, instead of writing for his keep as had been agreed.

A Wicklowman I know has brought the word back from the oil rigs of the North sea. He uses it as an adjective. 'Come on,' he said to me, 'leave that fordel work; it will be there for you when you get back.' Fordel work, he explained, was work that needn't be done immediately.

Sure enough, the dialect dictionaries have the word. It means to store up, to hoard for the future, according to the most reliable of them. *Fordel rent* is rent paid in advance, and *fordling* is a stock or provision for the rainy day.

There are many Wicklowmen working out of Aberdeen on the oil rigs and I wonder will all the good Scots words they pick up ever be assimilated into the rich language of their county. At any rate this *fordel*, sometimes *fardel* and *furdel*, is the same word as Middle English *fordele*, advantage. The Dutch word it came from is *voordeel*, advantage, furtherance.

Wicklow has absorbed many words from the older English, as well as from the Norse, Norman French and Irish. It's some years now since I saw an over-horsed young man, poncing for the benefit of the lady members of the Bray Hunt, go arse over head into a dyke filled with cold, swift-flowing water, near Barndarrig. An onlooker, a local farmer, called the dyke a *gool*.

*Gool*, sometimes *gull* as John Clare has it, is defined by the dialect dictionaries of England as a watercourse; a ditch. English readers please note that in Ireland a ditch is not a dyke; it is a bank that separates fields. A rider often has to negotiate a dyke or gool (an English ditch) on either side of it. Anyway, *gool* is found mainly in England's North Country, and it was brought there, and into Ireland, by the Normans, who had *goule*, mouth of an animal, a word they borrowed from medieval Latin *gula*, as found in *gula fluvii*, the mouth of a stream or river. I'm sure the young fellow we fished from the Wicklow gool would have been pleased at the time to be told that.

## Looby – Nightmare and Daymare

'A noun common enough in Antrim where I grew up was *looby*,' writes a Greystones woman,who wants to remain anonymous. 'Not loopy,' she emphasises, 'although used as an adjective it meant the same thing or near enough to it. A looby was a fool, an *amadhaun*; a looby person wasn't the full shilling. My husband thinks that this word comes from the Irish *lúb*, a twist, knot. Is he right?'

No. A good old word it is, though. Piers Plowman has it (1377): 'Grete lobyes and longe that lothe were to swynke'. (To swynke was to work hard). The Dublinman, Stanyhurst, in his *Description of Ireland* (late 16th-century) has: 'Sir you take me short, as long and as verie a lowbie as you imagine to make me'. As to its origin, there seems to be general agreement that the word is Germanic. There are many similar Teutonic words denoting clumsiness, and they live in the Danish *lobbes*, a clown, bumpkin, and in the Norwegian *lub*, *lubba*, a small, very corpulent person. Related, too, to the modern English *lubber*.

Kate O'Sullivan is ten. She asks me not to say where she lives, because, she says, her friends would give her a hard time for asking where the word *nightmare* comes from. Her mother told her to write to me. Kate also wants to know if there's such a word as *daymare*.

About 800 years ago, Kate, people believed that a nasty little goblin, called *mare* or *maer* in Old English, used to sit on people at night and bounce up and down on them while they slept, trying either to suffocate them or to give them frightening dreams. The word *mare* came to England, and to Ireland, from Germany and Scandinavia. It travelled far. The Norwegians 'called the goblin *mara,* the Pole's *zmora*; and the French invented the word *cauchemar* for nightmare.

You are a bit young yet to read Chaucer's *Canterbury Tales,* written over 600 years ago, because the English is a bit hard for one thing; but there is a prayer in one of the stories which is nice: 'Jesu Criste, and Seint Benedight, Bless this house fro the nighte-mare.' Terrible speller, wasn't he?

There is no such word as daymare, Kate, as far as I know. Maybe there should be. Anyway, thanks for the nice letter and for the two kisses. Here are three in return – x.x.x – from your friend.

## The Language of Kilkenny

*The Language of Kilkenny,* by Seamus Moylan, is a 400-page wonder of a book, its author's memorial, no matter what else he produces from his cloister in University College, Galway in the years ahead. I don't know Thomastown-born Dr Moylan, but I sincerely hope that he will be spoken of with reverence on the banks of the Barrow, Nore and Suir.

Most of this fascinating book is taken up with a 290-page lexicon. Consider these words:

*Glorags*: The buttocks. Moylan does no more than ask us to compare the Irish *glár,* soft mass, and Dinneen's *meall a larag,* his posteriors. Neither have I ever come across *vage,* found in the phrase 'to make a vage', to go on a voyage or journey. This is from Old French *veiage*; modern French is *voyage.*

I've learned that in Callan a *rustic* is a type of baker's loaf, a 'turnover'. In Graiguenamanagh, *saffron* means (or meant) 'sheep droppings, used in a cure for measles and whooping cough'. Dinneen and Ó Dónaill have *cróch,* saffron, and Dinneen tells us that *cróch na gcaorach,* juice of sheep droppings, steeped, was given to children suffering from measles. God Almighty!

*Telemachus* is the Kilkennyman's 'clamour or outcry; hullabaloo, bedlam'. Was the reasonably mild-mannered, son of Odysseus and Penelope responsible for this word? How in God's name did it surface in Glenpipe near Tullogher? A hedge schoolmaster's word?

The book preserves some of the lovely language of the three great rivers. *Ceatú*: 'The Dark Drift'. This drift coincides with the last quarter of the moon and the hour before the stop of the tide. It is an excellent drift for catching salmon. So, Irish survives on the dark waters. *Stiúir in aghaidh*, literally rudder against, is a call by a cot fisherman to direct the boat into the breeze. *Téagar* is the strong pull on a fishing net which indicates that a big fish has been netted. 'There's no téagar on it'; hence a poor catch – or none at all – is to be expected. The word in Irish means substance, strength. A *slack* is spent salmon. *Aingiril* and *angaire* are other Kilkenny words for it. Irish? Moylan is not sure. He's found *sleaingir* in Connemara.

I've mentioned only the lexicon. There are also sections on semantics and structures which may have a slightly less popular appeal. But for the 290-page lexicon alone all those interested in Anglo-Irish speech should have this treasure of a book on their shelves.

## Poke – Quiddy – Morth – Drutheen

A reader from Monaghan, who asks for anonymity, wants to know whether the word *poke*, a bag, sack, a wallet or a pocket, comes from the Irish *póca*.

Both *poke* and *póca* are from Old Norse *poki*, a bag, and both the English and Irish words are independent offspring. Chaucer refers to a pig in a poke in the *Canterbury Tales*, but by his time the word was common in the Scots language. No doubt the word travelled from Scotland to the north of Ireland.

I have often wondered how many of the compounds based on poke travelled across the waters of the Moyle. The Scots have *poke-brass*, pocket money; *poke-piece*, a keepsake coin; *poke-pudding*, a pudding boiled in a bag, a sausage, also a contemptuous name for an Englishman; and *poke-shakings*, the last and inferior flour shaken out of the sack, also figuratively, the youngest child of a family. Interestingly, in Donegal they have the Irish phrase *craitheadh an phocáin*, which is a direct translation of poke-shaking. Seán Mac Meanmain, God rest him, used the phrase as the title of his !ast book.

June Rogers, a Waterford woman, she tells me, wrote from Newmarket, the home of English racing, to ask me about a word her mother-in-law used. She has never heard it elsewhere, and it is a mystery to all her friends. The word is *quiddy*, and the old lady, who was a little hard of hearing, would say: 'Sorry, speak up. Quiddy?'

I have never come across this, but the EDD has. It is the French *que dis tu?*, what do you say? in disguise.

Back home again, this time to Antrim, from where a shy Glensman sent me the interesting word *morth*, which means plenty. So that you'd hear of a morth of hay, the result of a good summer, and a morth of cold, a heavy cold. Again, this word is a gift of our Scandinavian friends; it comes form the Old Norse *mergth*, plenty, abundance.

*Drutheen* is a word sent to me by a West Cork woman who tells me that she is too bashful to have her name recorded in print. A drutheen is a snail, and this it is spelled by Crofton Croker in his *Fairy Legends and Traditions*. 'A small white slug or naked snail, sought by young people on May Morning, which, if place on a slate covered with flour, described, it is believed, the initials of their sweetheart.' This is the Irish *drúchtín*. *Drúcht* is dew.

## Chiller – Holy Ground

Patricia Rainey, writing from Exeter, tells me that her father, who came from Co. Antrim, often used the word *chiller* for a double chin.

The form as Patricia gives it is, or was, used only in the north of Ireland; in Scotland and the north of England it is still *chuller* and *choller*, in Devon and its neighbouring counties *cholly*.

Yes, the chiller etc. was the fat flesh hanging from the lower jaw of man or beast; a dewlap; a double chin.

Chillers, chollers, etc. are also the gills of a fish in the southern counties of England, and the wattles of a cock or turkey-cock in Antrim and Down. There is no problem with the word's origin: Old English *ceolur*, the throat. Old High German has *chelero*, the throat, dewlap.


A Cork correspondent, Claire Nyhan, was annoyed recently by an English friend who asked innocently why Cork people have hijacked the term *the holy ground*. Surely, says Claire, the holy ground is Cobh; the song proves it.

The song, a stór, does no such thing, and some 19th-century broadsides I've seen place this particular holy ground in Bristol, adjacent to the docks. It was a red light district. Such districts all over the English-speaking world, including the west side of New York, and the waterfronts of Philadelphia and Halifax, Nova Scotia, were known as holy grounds. The term is now obsolete, I'm told.

The original holy ground was the notorious Seven Dials district of the parish of St Giles in London. Tom Moore, in *Tom Crib's Memorial* (1819), remarks that the term came from a celebrated fancy chant, or brothel song, ending every verse thus: 'For we are the boys of the Holy Ground, And we'll dance upon nothing (be hanged) and turn around.' 'Holy' is an obvious pun on 'Saint' Giles.

Eric Partridge tells us that an early explanation (1821) stated that the name 'is in compliment to the superior purity of its Irish population'. Ah, yes indeed! Many of the most notorious madams of the Seven Dials were Irish, and some of them, with touching patriotism, employed only Irish girls in their houses. Fine girls they were, by all accounts.


## Shocking – Shock – Reel Foot

'I have a few shocks for you,' writes James Gilmartin from London's North Kensington, originally from Kilkenny. 'Why do Irish people say things like "I feel shockin' bad"or worse still, "She's a shockin' nice girl"? You'd never hear an English person say the like.'

Indeed you would, James. *Shocking* is commonly used as an intensive all over England from Yorkshire to the southern shires. Let me give you some examples, all from Joe Wright's monumental EDD: 'I was astonished to find what a shocking nice taste it had' (Isle of Wight). 'He was quiet shocking (exceedingly quiet) and wouldn't hurt a fly' (Isle of Man). 'Ther' wull be a shockin' bad crop o' turmuts (turnips) if us dwoant get zome raain' (Berkshire). 'He took ill hisself wi' burn-gout: tormented him shocklin' cruel' (Devon).

Of course, this intensive is found all over Ireland, too. In the north it is found as a noun in the phrase 'my shockin!' – an exclamation. Lyttle, read more for the dialect than for any other reason nowadays, I suspect, wrote in *Paddy McQuillan*, 'A katched her at last, an' my shockin'! if she dinnae kick an' squeal an' struggle.' From Old French *choc*, from *choquier*, to make violent contact with. Undoubtedly of Germanic origin, related to Middle High German *schoc*.

The other *shock* referred to by Mr Gilmartin is sometimes spelled *shoch, shough, sheoch, and shaugh*. It means a puff of the pipe, a smoke. It is still used in all four provinces as a noun. In Ulster it is also found as a verb. Seamus MacManus of Donegal in his whimsical *The Bend of the Road* (1898) has, 'Himself and the Playboy shoughed out o' the same pipe.' This is the Irish *seach*, a turn; Dinneen has 'seach tobac', a smoke of a pipe.

Mary Grace, writing from Kilkenny, asks about her mother's expression *reel foot*. A reel foot is a deformed foot, thought by our superstitious ancestors to be induced by walking in pregnancy over a grave. I was aware of this term (and of its Irish antecedent) from manuscripts sent by schoolmasters in the 1930s and 1940s to the Irish Folklore Commission. It seems to have been common all over Leinster and Ulster, and I notice that it is included in the new *Concise Ulster Dictionary*, which does not venture an etymology. *Reel* is a corruption of the Irish *reilig*, a grave; the full Irish phrase for the deformity being *cam reilige (cam* means crooked; *reilige* is genitive of *reilig*, in case your Irish is rusty).

# Travel — Fwid

Mary O'Reilly is a Cavan woman who has been living in New York for twenty years. During a visit home this year she heard an expression that jogged her memory. She had offered a couple a lift home from Mass, but they declined, saying that as the day was fine they would *travel*. 'In my day,' said Mary, 'to travel meant to walk; I wonder is this found elsewhere in Ireland?'

To judge by an entry in the EDD this usage is found in Scotland and England as well as in the northern counties of Ireland. An Antrim correspondent sent 'I travelled it every fut o' the way' to Oxford.' From Down, another man wrote 'Are you goin' to travel or go by train?' And from Cavan a correspondent sent 'I travelled into town but Pat drove there.' The EDD recorded this from Cornwall: 'Will ye take a ride? No, I'll travel.' Our own beleaguered travellers were so called that because they once *walked* the country-side. They were called *an lucht siúil,* the walking people, in Irish; *shoolers* in the English of Ireland.

Mary's usage echoes the 14th-century *travaillen,* to make a journey, itself from Old French *travillier,* to undergo exertion. Travelling wasn't much fun in those days.

Jane McGettigan asks about a word common enough in Fanad, Co. Donegal. She recently heard a mother telling a daughter who was going to a dance: 'If that fella comes near you, be off in a *fwid,* do you hear me?'

The word is found in the dialect dictionaries under *whid, fud* and *whud,* and is glossed as 'a rapid, noiseless movement; a whisk, a quick run, a hasty flight, especially used of a hare'. Burns has 'Morning poussie whidden seen' and a lesser Scots poet, Smart, remembered more for his dialect than for his rhymes, has 'The lintie (linnet) whids amang the whins.'

There is another, unrelated whid, and I've heard this, as *fud,* used by old timers who live at the back of Muckish, near Falcarragh. To them it meant a tall tale, a fib. Again, this is a Scots word, and Rhymer Rab frae Ayrshire has 'Ev'n Ministers they hae been kenned In holy rapture, A rousing whid at times to vend.' This whid is related to the Old English *cwide,* a statement, proverb, saying; but as for Miss McGettigan's word, it earlier meant a blast of wind, and it blew our way from Scandinavia. Compare the Old Icelandic *hvitha*, a squall.

## Sweet Fanny Adams – Cat – The Devil

An anonymous reader, whose epistle has a Thurles postmark, asks about the phrase, *Sweet Fanny Adams*. 'Is it true,' my correspondent asks, 'that sweet Miss Adams's initials were anagrammed into a vulgar phrase, or is the other theory correct: that sweet Fanny Adams is simply that vulgar phrase laundered so as to be accepted in polite society?'

Well, poor Miss Adams, did exist. Her life was short and sad. She came from Alton in Hampshire and she was murdered and dismembered in 1867 at the age of eight by a mad accountant. Unfortunately, her remains turned up in a trunk in the Deptford Navy Yard precisely at the time when tinned meat was being introduced as the staple food of a reluctant Royal Navy. No sweeties for guessing what the sailors called what they were now expected to like or lump.

Subsequently, the term was used to cover anything that was valueless. As for the vulgar phrase, it is of far more recent origin.

Many of the phrases we modern landlubbers use come from the speech of the old-time sailors. I had always thought that 'not enough room to swing a cat' was first used in reference to the cat-o'-nine-tails, but according to the naval historians, Bill Beavis and Richard McCloskey, in their fascinating *Salty Dog Talk* (London, 1983), this may not be so. You see, the cat was also the name for a sailling collier common throughout northern Europe at one time. They were very 'handy' vessels: Captain Cook's *Endeavour* was formerly a Northumberland cat. ' But they were also very small, about 600 tons: and our two historians think that the expression referred to a port or anchorage which would not have enough room for this small vessel to swing at anchor.

'Between the devil and the deep sea' is another expression of nautical origin. The seams between a ship's planks had to be repacked with oakum and pitch to prevent leakage, and the *devil* was the outside seam of the deck planks, nearest the scuppers. It was very difficult to pitch, due to the spray washing over the side: hence its name. In foul weather, as well, a man could easily be knocked over by a sea and washed into the scuppers, finding himself literally between the devil seam and the deep sea. 'The devil to pay' originally ran 'the devil to pay and no hot pitch'. Same devil; to *pay* meant to caulk, and can be traced to Old High German *pëh*, pitch.

## Coup Carley – Impudence

May McClintock of Glendooen Rectory, New Mills, Letterkenny, writes: 'We all know in Donegal how to coup carley: every child can do it. But I would like to know the origin of the term.'

For the benefit of people in the south to *coup carl* or *coup carley* means to turn a somersault, to go head over heels. Coup, sometimes written *cowp*, is found all over Scotland and northern England, as well as in Ulster. It means to upset, capsize, overturn. 'But stooks were cowpet wi' the blast,' wrote Burns. Scott's pal, Hogg, in his *Tales*, has: 'If he hadna been ta'en unawares I wadna hae been coupit sae easily.' Hence we get the phrases *to coup off*, to fall off; *to coup over*, to fall asleep or to be confined in childbed; *to coup the creels*, to turn head over heels, to die, to have a love-child. As to the word's origin the great dictionaries hedge their bets, but I think it may be related to Old French *coup* from Late Latin *colpus*, from Latin *colaphus*, from Greek *kólaphos*, a slap, a smack.

Now what of *carley*? This is a form of *carl*, a fellow, a man, a word Chaucer knew: he has 'The Miller was a stout carl for the nones' in the *Canterbury Tales*. The word is from Old Norse *karl*, man. So that to coup carley means simply to turn the man over, to go head over heels or do a cartwheel.

James Hanley, a Dublin man who now lives near Canterbury, wrote to tell me of a word used by his mother, who died at eighty over twenty years ago. The word was *impudence*, but to the old lady it meant not impertinence, or disrespect, but indecency.

Cotgrave has this meaning, 'from French *impudence,* shamelessness, from Latin *impudens*'. A few years before the great lexicographer's time Shakespeare has Helena say in *All's Well That Ends Well*: 'Tax of impudence, A Strumpet's boldness'. The EDD quotes from an English diocesan register of 1682, which records the shock of somebody who reported to the bishop seeing a couple engaged in outrageous tally-ho: 'This deponent, blushing to see soe much impudence between the said persons, immediately went out of the same chamber.'

I hope Mrs Hanley's usage didn't die with her. It has been in English since the 14th century. Does it survive anywhere in Ireland? Collins says that it is obsolete across the water.

## Bairn – Cowl

The word *bairn* is common is Scotland, the north of Ireland and the northern counties of England, where it is often spelled 'barn', as it was in Piers Plowman long, long ago: 'Tho this barn was ybore there blased a sterre.' Ruth Rogers from Derry asks about its origin.

Bairn, as any Ulster person will tell you, is a child. From it, the Scots have given us the compounds *bairn-ailments*, children's illnesses; *bairn-bairn*, a grandchild; *bairn-bed*, the womb; *bairn-part*, inheritance; *bairn-clarts*, children's sweetmeats; *biarn-skep*, a shallow basket for baby linen.

In England's north country, however, a bairn is a female child, a girl. *Notes and Queries,* back in 1867, says: 'I remember an old gentleman in the East Riding of Yorkshire exclaiming, when his first grandchild, a girl, was born, 'It's nobbu a bairn!' – meaning to express his disappointment at its not being a boy.'

'Bless us, barn!' is an expression still used in Leeds, though I'm told that most of the people who use it have forgotten its origin. The barn was, of course, the child Jesus.

At any rate, *bairn/barn* is from Old English *bearn,* a son or daughter.

J. Power from Ferrybank, a Co. Kilkenny suburb of Waterford, once heard the word *cowl* used by a fisherman in Dunmore East. The cowl was a wicker basket for holding fish. My correspondent wants to know if the word is Irish. No. Its origin is Old English *cawel*, a basket,

*Cowl* is also a dialect word for a tub of water. It, too, travelled here from England, probably on the fishing boats. This word is not from *cawel*, but from Middle English *covelle*, from Old French, *cuvele*, from Latin *cupella*, the diminutive of *cupa*, a cask.

There is another cowl that smells of the sea, a word that has intrigued me since I first heard it from my friend Jack Devereux in Kilmore Quay twenty years ago. This cowl Jack glossed as the innards of a fish. I thought it might be related to Irish *cabhail*, body, torso, but I now find that the Cornish fishermen know cowls as fish bladders. They also use the verb to cowl, to scrape out fish guts; to scrape scales, guts, etc., from the deck: 'Cowl the deck and then scrub it.' The verb is of French origin. Cotgrave, the great 17th-century lexicographer, gives us *cueillir*, to gather, to cull.

## Bladdock — Carlin — Garrane-bane — Stevin

Jane Beare, who lives in Belfast, and who is interested in the braid Scots of the north, wrote to ask if I can throw light on two words from Co. Down. The first is *bladdoch*, a sovereign cure for a hangover, according to her grandfather. This word is found in various forms in the north of Ireland, in Scotland, and as far away as the Orkneys and Shetland. It comes from the Gaelic *bláthach*, buttermilk.

Jane's second word is *carlin,* a disparaging term for an old woman. Burns had this word. He refers to 'shaking hands wi' wabster loons, And kissing barefit carlins' (a wabster is a weaver). The Scots also have the compounds *carlin-cat,* she-cat; *carlin-teuch,* hardy, tough as an old woman. The oldest reference in Scots literature to carlin is in Dalrymple, *Leslie's History of Scotland* (1597): 'Sum ald carlingis, sworne to witchcraft.' The word is from Old Norse *kerling,* a woman, used almost always of an old woman.

From Co. Down to Clonakilty where a woman of ancient lineage, as she describes herself, asks about the origin of her husband's favourite epithet, in constant use in connection with a politician he dislikes immensely. The favoured word is *garraun*; it means a gelding, and is from Irish *gearrán*, from *gearradh*, to cut. Carleton has it in *The Party Fight and Funeral* in the compound *garranebane*, which he glosses for us. His sentence is: 'Would you have me for to show the garrane-bane and lave them like a cowardly thraitor?' He explained: 'Garranebane, the white horse i.e. wanting in mettle. Tradition affirms that James the Second escaped on a white horse from the Battle of the Boyne, and from this circumstance a white horse has become a symbol of cowardice.'

'Wait your stevin, boy!' said an elderly lady in a pub in Wexford's Broadway (near enough to Rosslare) to a young fellow who had lost the run of himself and burst into song unasked, while a young woman who had been invited to sing was delicately clearing her throat in the approved manner. *Stevin* is my spelling (it rhymes with Kevin); I've never seen it written. What an old word it is, brought over by the followers of Fitzstephen and company from Pembrokeshire and other places over 800 years ago. *Stefyn* in Old English meant a period of time.

## Betimes — Cordon Blue — Butt — Bird

Not far from Borris in Co. Carlow I overheard an old timer saying goodnight to a friend with whom he had downed a pint or two. 'I must be off,' he said, 'it's all right for you but I must be up betimes.' I hadn't heard this *betimes*, which means early, in years. It is a Tudor survival, still common enough in England but as rare here in Ireland as policemen on Inis Oirr, I'm thinking. Shakespeare had it in *Antony and Cleopatra*: 'To business that we love we rise betime'; and in *Othello* he had: 'Betimes in the morning I will beseech the virtuous Desdemona.'

That other *betimes,* meaning at times, occasionally, is still as common as it was when P.J. MacCall wrote in the *Shamrock Magazine* over a hundred years ago: 'No wonder he do be so hard on the road contractors for the slaumin' he gets goin' these roads betimes.' (*Slaumin* is from Irish *Slám*, slime, dirt.)

Margaret Long from Killiney wrote to ask about the origin of *cordon bleu*, high cuisine and all that. Once upon a time 'un cordon bleu' signified a chevalier of the Order of the Holy Ghost. Under the Bourbons this outfit was regarded as the highest order of chivalry. The order's decoration was suspended from a blue ribbon. By all accounts the dinners eaten by these heroes were of such excellence that cordon bleu came to signify the very best in cooking, and cordon blue chefs the princes of the kitchen.

A *butt* is a type of cart. I know the word from west Cork, but it may be used in neighbouring Munster counties for all I know. At any rate, C. O'Driscoll from Macroom asks about the word's origin.

Well, it seems to have travelled from the south of England to us. Butts were and are used over there chiefly for carrying manure. In Somerset a butt-load was a load of about 18 cwt. Its origin is the Old Cornish *butt*, a dung-cart. The Welsh have *bwt* for the same vehicle. How the word came to West Cork is anybody's guess.

Finally, may I advise 'Bird fancier' from Bray that, *bird*, nowadays slang for a young woman, is older than he thinks, at least 500 years older. Once it meant a maiden, and he'll find 'But Mary byrde, thoue neyd not soo' in a play written about 1400. Swift called Vanessa a trim bird. Burns, who fancied the species to excess betimes, spelled the word *burd*, and Walter Scott has 'When in my arms burd Helen dropt.' Not his friend Helen Campbell, thankfully; judging from her portrait she was as broad in the beam as a Ballyvourney butt.

## Oose — Flourish — Cat-walk

Dermot Quirk from Grace O'Malley Road, Howth, tells me that his mother is from Kintyre in Scotland and that she has two words that baffle him. The first is *oose*. It means, he says, those little balls of wool that form on woollen jumpers.

Also written *ooze,* Mrs Quirk's word is still common in rural Scotland. *Oose* was glossed in Perth, in the days when ink was a dear commodity, as fluffy woollen material stuffed into an inkstand to prevent the ink from spilling. But where did the word come from? It is the plural of the Scots word *oo,* meaning wool. What language *oo,* or indeed its cousin *wool* for that matter, ultimately came from, nobody knows for sure. There are cognate words in most of the languages of Europe and many of those of India, dead and alive. It has a relation near home in the Irish *olann.*

Mr Quirk's letter goes on: 'the other word she uses is *flourish,* noun, meaning the blossom from a bush. I once brought her home some blossom from a cherry tree. She refused to have it in the house, saying that it was bad luck to bring flourish into a house.' Yes indeed, flourish is a lovely Scots noun, common too in Ulster, and the poet Thomson (*fl.* 1880) in his *Musings* wrote of 'the flourish on the tree that hings'. The Scots also have the adjective *flourished.* The earliest reference I can find is one from *The Complaynt of Scotlande* (1549): 'The borial blasts of the thre borouing dais of Marche had chaissit the fragrant flureis of euyrie frute tree far athourt the fieldis.'

And so to a letter from somebody who signs herself Model Girl. 'Tell us,' she says, 'where does the word *cat-walk* come from? Should we models use it? I mean, is it demeaning? I'm thinking of words like *cat-house,* if you get my meaning.'

Well now, the *cat* in cat-house is a word used in low speech since Chaucer's time. It's either from French *catin,* or from Dutch *kat,* a harlot. The *cat-walks* you adorn, Model Girl, originated in the brick-paved pathways, usually one brick or nine inches wide, laid down across the Flanders mud by British soldiers during the Great War. So called, I imagine, because only a cat could walk across them easily. I read somewhere that the models' *cat-walk* came into slang usage as late as the seventies. Grace, Ann, is this true?

# Corned — Gloss — Mow

A domestic discussion on the beef crisis led James Kenny of Raheny to write to me to enquire about the origin of the word *corned*. Why corn? asks Mr Kenny; after all, corned beef is beef that is pickled, slightly salted. Was corn once used in the salting process?

The history of the word *corned* is complicated, I fear. Bear with me.

Modern English *corn* is from Anglo-Saxon, *corn*. You'll find the same word in Old Frisian, Old High German and Old Saxon, while the Old Norse is *korn*. So far so good. But these words, not to mention the Germanic *kurnam* and the Gothic *kaurn* came originally from Indo-European *grnóm*, a worn-down particle; whence came the Latin *granum*, and the Old Irish *grán*, grain; the Greek *graus*, an old woman, and *geron*, an old man; the Sanskrit *ytryati*, wastes away, and *jirna*, wasted, old. From the same Indo-European spring came the verb *corn*, with its echo of the *gr* base, to make or become granular; to sprinkle with salt in grains, and so to preserve with salt, as in corned beef. A long journey, Mr Kenny.

'I was welcomed in a Donegal cottage last winter by a lovely old lady who asked me to sit and take a *gloss*. I thought she meant a glass, but it turned out that she had a sit-down by the fire in mind. Where does this expression come from?' Julia Kerins of Sutton, Co. Dublin, is my correspondent.

This *gloss* is an import from Scotland. I've heard it only once, and I recollect that gloss to the woman who used the word meant a very red fire. There is a Scottish word, *glossing*, which means blushes. Anyway, gloss came originally from the Old Norse *glossi*, a blaze. Gloss, a sheen, comes from the same source.

Finally, a lady from Warrenpoint who didn't sign her letter because of the nature of her query, she tells me, sent me the word *mow*, and tells me that in her day it did *not* mean to cut hay. It was not used in polite society, she says. Yes, I can imagine. The naughty word is still in use in Scotland and in England also. It's very old slang. In *Kitteis Confession*, a broadside from 1550, the young lady in question says 'Will Leno mowit me.' I've read the thing and

God's truth I'm still not sure whether she was complaining or boasting.

## Stampy – Candam – Cross Days

Thanks to Darina Allen for telling me that a *gabhlóg* is a prop used in east Cork kitchens to set the bastable at a correct height above an open fire. Darina would, I suspect, be better able than myself to answer a question sent by Ann Kelly of Youghal: 'Where does the word *stampy* come from, and what precisely is it?'

The Irish version is *steaimpí*, and Father Dinneen thought that the word was cognate with the Welsh *stwmp*, stomp. The Tailor of Gougane told Eric Cross that 'the old people would grate potatoes on a tin grater, and then squeeze them into a tub of water. From the water they would get the starch for their clothes. There was no such thing as a bastable in those days. The stampy was made on a bread tree, which was a kind of sloping board before the fire to hold the bread as you would make toast nowadays!' Stampy, a potato cake like boxty, has aphrodisiac powers, according to a west Cork song. Maybe this was what George Fitzmaurice had in mind when he wrote in his play, *The King of the Barna Men*, 'A strange thing occurred to myself a Friday night through taking my share of the stampy for supper.'

Speaking of Kerrymen, a friend tells me that not long ago he witnessed the acute embarrassment of a young man from Dublin who had come all the way to take the daughter of a north Kerry house out. The company had played cards, and the young man shared in the last pot. He rose to leave with his young woman, apparently forgetting his money, but he was told by mammy to be sure to take his *candam* with him. Yes, gentle leaders, the pronunciation is almost identical. The Kerry word, which means a share or part of something, comes originally from the Latin *quantum*. Stiofán Ó hAnnracháin has it in his great book, *Caint an Bhaile Dhuibh*, a collection of Irish words still used in an English-speaking north Kerry parish.

Looking at a list of Clare words and phrases found in the English of that county, and sent to me by their collector, Dr Patrick Henchy, I find *Lá Crosta na Bliana*. My friend's gloss is: 'Cross or contrary day of the year. Only the Irish form is used. The day of the week on which December 28th falls is regarded as an unlucky day for the following year. One would be loath to marry on that day, or to launch a new project.' Aye, or to eat stampy, girls. You have been warned. Be careful on Thursdays.

## Thole – Vennel – Annoy

The word *thole* is one of my favourite Ulster words. Of course, it's also a Scots word and a north of England dialect word. It means to bear, suffer, endure, tolerate. 'Me that can't thole the taste of whisky', said a liar in Hamilton's *Across an Ulster Bog* (1896). The *Bally-mena Observer* of 1892 has 'I can hardly thole the pain o' my finger.' Hence we find *tholeable,* bearable; *tholeless,* enervated, almost useless; *tholemoody*, patient. Catherine Kelly from Derry has tholed my long delay in answering her query about the origin of the word: it comes from Old English *tholian*, to suffer, endure, hold out.

I came across an interesting word recently when I was looking through that venerable scholarly journal, *Notes and Queries*. The word was *vennel*, and this is what a Strabane contributor had to say in 1879: 'In the town of Strabane, there are a number of narrow passages, called vennels, from the main street to the river shore, between or through the intervening houses. They are public rights of way, about six feet wide.'

The word has also been recorded in Scotland and in Yorkshire. I wonder is it still in use in Strabane? Have the vennels themselves disappeared? The word is the French *venelle*, a little street.

My inquiry as to whether the word *vennels* is still in use anywhere in Ireland brought some interesting letters. My thanks to Mrs R. Connolly of Brunswick Road, Bangor, who, informs me that The Vennel runs from Queen's Parade to King Street in her lovely town; and to Dr David Davin of Gilford, Craigavon, who remembers the word being used in his childhood in Derry. A vennel, he says, was 'the channel at the side of a country road, or even a town road beside the kerb (or *cribben* as it is known in Gilford) along which the surface water runs'.

Dr Davin also sent me an interesting local usage of *annoy*. 'When I first came to Gilford and heard patients say that they were annoyed, I used to get a bit defensive and wondered what I had done to upset them. I soon realised that they meant that they were worried.'

Dear me, what an old one this is. The Thornton MS of 1400 has 'thou erte anoyede aftire many thynges', *anoyede aftire* meaning worried about. Annoy in all its meanings has an interesting pedigree. It is from Old French *anoeir*, to weary, from Late Latin *inodiare*, from the Latin phrase *mihi in odio est*, it is hateful to me.

Seán Ó Donnagáin of Thornhill Road, Mount Merrion, Dublin, has sent me a collection of very interesting words from west Offaly. I quote him about one of them: 'When my brother and I were very young we would keep the greater part of our mug of tea for our special "game" after the food was eaten. The "game" consisted of keeping the rim of the mug to your mouth, but instead of swallowing the tea in a normal way, each mouthful was made to generate, with proper motion of the Adams's apple, a half-choking, half-gurgling sound on its way down. My mother would reprimand us with the command "Don't guttle your tea!" Years later, I came across the word *guthghaoil* in Dinneen's Dictionary, referring to the sound made by pigs. Ó Dónaill hasn't the word.'

Dare I say it? Dinneen was chancing his arm, Gaelicising the Offaly lady's imitative word. *Guttle* is found in Scotland and all over England. I can trace it no further back than a tract called *Horae Subsecivae*, printed in 1777 in Devon. My granddaughter has picked up the word *guttler* in school, in Cornwall.

## Chatter and Box

Margaret O'Brien from Limerick confesses to being a *chatterbox*. She wants to know the origin of the word.

*The chatter* part is as old as the 14th century and it is of imitative origin. In rural England to this day a chatterbox is also called a *chatterbag*, a *chattercan*, a *chattermag* and a *chatterbasket*; *chatter-water* is slang for weak tea.

The *box* part is a 16th-century colloquial word for mouth. It has survived in the earthy speech of English and Irish farmers as a word for the uterus of a cow or mare. The American usage of the word will be familiar to fans of African American rap music who use it just as the Bard of Stratford did. You may remember that in *All's Well That Ends Well* Parolles says to Bertram who has just married Helena but refuses to go to bed with her: 'To th' wars, my boy, to th' wars! He wears his honour in a box unseen, That hugs his kicky-wicky here at home Spending his manly marrow in her arms, Which should sustain the bound and high curvet Of Mars's fiery steed.'

All our boxes, decent or otherwise, come from late Old English *box*, a wooden receptacle, from Latin *pyxis*, from Late Greek *puxis*.


## Skite – Gibbet – Lachter

Mary Anne Kelly McMannus wrote from Venice, Florida, to ask about the word *skite*, or *skyte*, which she remembers from her youth in Bailieborough, Co. Cavan. To skyte, like to jap, meant to splash.

*Skite* is common all over the north of Ireland, Scotland and northern England, as verb and noun. 'To save oorsels frae the rain that was skytin' doon', recorded in Lanarkshire, echoes Mary Anne's meaning. Skyte also means a sharp, passing shower; a splash or jap of water put in whiskey; diarrhoea in animals. Burns has 'When hailstones drive wi' bitter skyte.' Skyte here means a blow delivered sideways. Lyttle has 'Gied the hearth a bit skite wi' the besom' from Co. Down. The dialect dictionaries and glossaries don't give an etymology, but I'm pretty sure that all the above skytes are ultimately based on the Old Norse *skyt*, to shoot.

Pat Cullen of Santry, who tells me that he was reared near Carnew, asks where the south Wicklow and Wexford word, *jibbets*, sometimes spelled *gibbets*, comes from.

Always a plural, the word means smithereens, scraps, morsels. Patrick Kennedy in *Evenings in the Duffrey* (1869) has: 'They'd have made gibbets of him only for Tony Whitty.'

William Cobbett had the word *gibbet* for a small load of corn or hay. Cobbett's word is from Old French *gibe*, packet or bale. But the Wicklow/Wexford words are, believe it or not, related to Old French *gibet*, the gallows, literally little cudgel, from *gibe*, cudgel, itself a word of uncertain origin.

Willie O'Kane from Dungannon once sent me the splendid phrase *cuckoo's lachter*, by which is meant an only child. I mentioned the expression in this column a few years ago. I wrote then that lachter was the Irish *lachtar*, a clutch of eggs, which is right, as far as it goes. The trouble is, it doesn't go far enough.

I have now found out that the word is found all over the neighbouring island in a variety of spellings: *laughther, lachter, letter, lawter, lochter, lauchter* among them. All these, and the Irish word, are from Old Norse *latr*, also *latir*, the place where animals lay their young.

## Shive – Slawher – Lace

The young man from near Campile in south Wexford, hungry after a day's fishing, asked his mother for a *shive* of bread, even though the dinner was almost cooked. *Shive* is a word once widely used in Ireland, and common, too, all over the neighbouring island. It means a cut, a slice, a round of bread. 'A shive of a cut loaf is never missed' is a Lancashire version of the unrespectable aphorism. 'To give the loaf and have to beg the shive' is a phrase from Yorkshire. It means to give away one's property and then to have to beg a pittance from the person who got it.

A good friend of mine from south-east Wexford, whose mother also used 'a shive of bread', wants to know whether the word is related to the barony of Forth word *sive*, the implement once used in cutting hay, a *scythe* to the rest of us.

*Shive* is ultimately from the Norse *skifa*, a slice; whereas *scythe*, and the dialect *sive*, are from Old English *sigthe*, related to Old Norse *sigthr*. But go back to Old God's time and you'll find the probable origin of all those words in the Indo-European *sek*, cut (think of *section*). I wonder did the American slang word *shiv*, a knife, from Romany *chiv*, blade, come ultimately from the same ancient source?

From Tom Ryan, a Tipperaryman who has lived in Dublin for half a century, comes an inquiry about some of the words used in his youth. Tom's first word is *slawher*. His mother, when she had to leave the children to go to market or to Mass would say, 'You'll have to slawher for yourselves while I'm gone.' This is Irish *soláthar*, to make provision for, to fend for.

Tom's second word is the verb *to lace*, to beat. 'The master laced the arse of him' is Tom's example of how the word was used. He also gives the word as a noun: 'He got the father and mother of a lacing.'

This is the Irish *léasadh*, a flogging, but I think I should qualify that statement. You see, to lace and lacing are also found all over England, from Yorkshire to Cornwall. The EDD has 'I'll lace thee till thee kissent stand' from Devon, and 'He could lace all the chaps in the place at runnin', from Staffordshire.

Both the Irish and the English words come, independently perhaps, from the Old French *laz*, from Latin *laqueus*, a noose.

## Boon — Bawd

In almost every collection of words made north of a line between Louth and Mayo, I have found the word *boon*, a band of reapers, shearers, turf-cutters; voluntary help given to a farmer by his neighbours. The origin of the words more often than not is given as Irish *buíon*, a band, a group. Not so, I'm afraid.

A boon was service, formerly given in kind or in labour, paid by a tenant to his landlord, or, as Cotgrave's great dictionary of the early 17th century has it, 'a toilsome and drudging daies work lent unto a friend or more properly due by a vassal or tenant'. The word is still common in the north of Ireland and in Scotland, where one also finds *boon dinner*, a meal given in the harvest field to the combined harvester men and their helpers. *Boon ploughing* still goes on in Ayrshire and in the northern counties of England, where once, we are told, 'the day ended in jollity, the recipient of help from his neighbours finding entertainment for all'.

The oldest reference to this custom, the equivalent of our Irish *meitheal*, is from the Nottingham of 1494, where a man wrote in his little accounts book: 'Item, for bred to the boners att Epurstenour for castyng erth ...'

Boon is from Old Norse *bon*, request. It is related to the Old English *ben*, a prayer, as in *ben-rip*, the service of reaping gratuitously.

'I wonder what would be said nowadays to a man who never tired of having a *bawd* for his supper?', asks Mrs Jane Armstrong of Bangor. The good lady's father, who came frae Ballymoney, had this old word for a hare.

Shakespeare plays on this sense in *Romeo and Juliet*. '*Mercutio:* A bawd, a bawd, a bawd! So ho! *Romeo:* What hast thou found? *Mercutio*: No hare, sir.'

Bawd and bacon was a favourite dish in 18th-century Scotland. Burns refers to it somewhere; for the life of me I can't remember where. A line in a spirited song of 1785 has: 'I saw and shame it wis to see You rin awa like bawds.'

Have bawd, hare and bawd, whore, a common ancestor? Yes, I feel sure that both come from Old French *baude*, proud. The French word is of Germanic origin. There is, for instance, the Old High German *bald*, and Old English *beald* meaning bold.

## Because Why – Citóg – Thropple

The adverbial phrase *because why* is bothering June Fitzgerald of Waterford. She wants to know if it is an Irishism, and secondly, is it one confined to parts of her native county.

I've heard it in Carlow and in Wexford, but it is to be heard as well in the southern counties of England. It means, of course, because, for the reason that. It's in the 18th-century Dublin song *The Night afore Larry was Stretched*: 'because why his courage was high'. Crofton Croker has it too in his *Legends* from Munster: 'Quite melancholy because why the river was flooded and he couldn't get across.'

It's an old phrase. It was first recorded in a manuscript from *c*.1305: 'I prey the take hit nouht in greve. Bi cause whi hit is clerkes wise.'

'Don't let that kitter-handed ass tune yur car,' said a man to an Armagh correspondent, Ruth Warke, recently. She wants to know the origin of *kitter-handed*.

I first heard this expression from Willie O'Kane of Dungannon. The EDD has *katty-handed* from Ayrshire. 'It was very incommodious for me to be on the left side, as I have been all my days katty-handed,' was recorded in 1820.

Well, you have the Irish *ciotach* and the Classical Irish *cittach*, meaning both left-handed and awkward. Of course, there's the cognate *ciotóg*, Irish English *kithogue*, used by Carleton and a host of other 19th-century Irish novelists, and by Joyce in *Ulysses*. It means a left-handed person. *Ciotógaí* (Irish English *kithogey*), a term of disparagement for an untidy workman, was recorded in the English of north Kerry by Stiofán Ó hAnnracháin.

Should we look no further than Irish, then? Well, you see, there is a Norse connection further back. There is the North Frisian *käitig*, lefthanded, and *kei*, awkward; the Swedish dialect *kitja*, the left hand; *kaj-händ*, sinister.

From a visitor from Fermanagh I heard the word *thrapple* recently, 'As long as a goose's thrapple,' he said. You'll find this word, and *thropple*, all over the north, and in Scotland, as well. It means the windpipe. Hence you'll find *open-throppled*, fond of a jar; *thropple-deep in claber*, up to the neck in mud; *thropple-girth*, a tie or cravat, a hunter's stock.

We find 'throppil: iugulum', in a glossary from 1570. The Old English has *throt-bolla*, gullet or windpipe.

# Words That Went Wrong

To *cant* in many parts of Ireland means to sell by auction, and a lady who lives in Birr wonders what the origin of the word is.

I've been having my own problems with this word recently, wondering whether I should include it in a dictionary of Irish words found in the English of Ireland. You'll find *ceant* in the Irish dictionaries, but it is certainly a borrowing from English.

Cant is still used in many parts of England, and is now regarded as a dialect word. Swift has: 'They were everywhere canting their land upon short leases,' in his *Modest Proposal*. Carleton, in *Fardorougha the Miser*, speaks of a man who 'canted all the world we had at half price and turned us to starve upon the world'. Crofton Croker, in early 19th-century Cork, wrote: 'He'll cant every ha'porth we have'; and Anna Maria Hill and her husband, writing a little later, said of an unfortunate household in the south-east that 'every haporth upon the lands and the house was canted'.

*Cant/ceant* are from Old French *inquant*, which is from medieval Latin *in quantum* for how much.

'How old is *daft*?', asks Joan Burke of Limerick. Quite old. Its origin is Old English *gedaefte*, gentle, modest, retiring.

Like so many old words it has changed its meaning utterly over the centuries. *Wench* was once the lovely Old English *wencel*, a child; in an early poem the Blessed Virgin calls herself God's *wench*. *Lewd* once simply meant ignorant, unlearned. *Tinsel* has fallen on hard times; this, the French *étincelle*, once meant anything that sparkles, so that cloth of tinsel was cloth inwrought with silver and gold. *Tawdry* was once the finery, beautiful lace and the like, that could be bought at the fair of St Audrey or Etheldreda. *Voluble* once meant fluent, turning readily, from Latin *volubilis*, from *volvere*, to turn; and *leer* was once the Old English *hléor*, the cheek. *Specious* in the 14th century meant fair, from Latin *speciousus*, plausible. And, as Archbishop Trench once asked in a famous sermon, could the Magdalen have ever bequeathed us *maudlin* in its present contemptuous application, if the tears of penitential sorrow had been held in due honour by the world?

'They speak a very rich English in west Clare, due to a large extent to its Irish background,' writes Mary O'Brien, an exile from the Banner county in our 33rd county, Kilburn, in London. She goes on to ask where the word *quingled* comes from. It means married, she explains.

Both Dr Patrick Henchy and the late Pádraic Collins sent me the Irish word *cuingeal* many moons ago, as it has long been assimilated into the English of Clare.

Both Dinneen and Ó Dónaill have it. Dr Henchy says that in his part of Clare it originally meant a yoke that ties two goats together by the neck. That's where Mary's word came from, without a doubt. A good word. Maybe they'd now consider writing it into the Constitution.

'Have you the word *wheen* down south?', asks my valued correspondent, Jack Bell from Bangor. It means 1. A few, a number, several. 2. A good deal, some, somewhat.

Bram Stoker of Dracula fame has the word in *The Snake's Pass*. He heard it in Mayo: 'I've heard a wheen of quare things in me time.' Apart from that, I've never come across it in the south, but it may well be alive and well in the border counties for all I know. Moira O'Neill in her *Songs of the Glens of Antrim* (1900) has: 'There's a wheen things that used to be an' now has had their day.' And Savage-Armstrong in his *Ballads of Down* wrote, in 1901: 'Ye may hae won A wheen o' honour 'nayth the sun.' The word is from Old English *hwene*, somewhat, a little.

'He's *trig* as they come.' Monica Nolan from Sutton heard this used by an Ulsterman at gun-dog trials last year. I'm not surprised. It is common in Scotland. It means reliable, faithful. Trig in Donegal and in Wexford means spruce, in good order. Seumus MacManus in *The Bend in the Road* has 'There, me man, is yer boot, as thrig an' as nate as Toal-a-Gallacher can make it.' A Wexfordman who farms near Carne complained to me last year about his wife's ducks soiling his stable yard. 'How can I keep the blessed place trig with them', was his olagón. The word travelled to America as well.

You may remember e.e. cummings's poem in which a 'trig Westpointer, most succinctly bred', tortured a soldier with a heated bayonet. Both Monica's and cummings's trigs have a common ancestor in the Old Norse *tryggr*, true.

## Shiffin – Rap – Ravishing

Not since the O'Tooles and the O'Byrnes lost everything in the early 17th century has Irish been widely spoken in that part of Wicklow known to us as Glenroe. Still, it is amazing how many good Irish words survive in the speech of the people who live around Kilcoole. Just after the game against Mexico, a man turned to me and said, 'We're leanin' on shiffins now.' When I tell you that a *shiffin* is a stalk of straw, you'll know what he meant. It is the Irish *sifín* in disguise.

In folklore you'll find 'the night of the shiffins', and 'the day of the shiffins', and thereby hangs a good tale about the bould Dan O'Connell. The story goes that the great man boasted that he could raise Ireland in a day. On the night called *oíche na sifín*, from a house near Derrynane, a man went forth from his house carrying a *sifín* to the next house. That man was told to pull a *sifín* from his own thatch and to go to the next house; and so on, each man going to the nearest house to his own. Thus word was passed around Ireland in one night.

A lady from Ballyshannon who doesn't want to be named, for a reason which will become obvious, tells me that her sixteen-year-old daughter frightened the life out of some American visitors recently when she came home late from a date to announce that she was ravished. *Ravished* in many parts of the north means highly delighted. Seumus MacManus, in his *Bold Blades of Donegal*, has 'A ravished man was that marchant to give Billy his roll of tibaccy – and equally ravished was Billy to tie it to the right side of his saddle.' To ravish, in the sense to fill with delight, is old, but I'm not sure exactly how old. Addison has it: 'My friend was ravished with the beauty, innocence, and sweetness that appeared in all their faces.' It survives in phrases such as 'a ravishing beauty', and such is the way of the world of words that the Ballyshannon girl's ravishment is from the same source as that verb which means to carry off by force, to rape. (Old French *raviss-*, stem of *ravir*, from vulgar Latin *rapire*, from Latin *rapere*, to seize.)

Finally, Miss S. Fitzsimons from Drumbracken, Co. Monaghan, wants to know the origin of the word *rap*, in the phrases 'not worth a rap', and 'not to give a rap'. It was a counterfeit copper coin in use in the 18th century. It was first mentioned in print by Swift in 1724, in *Drapier's Letters*.

## The Hungry Grass — Led-will — Libe

Not a few of the old people I once knew believed in the *féar gortach,* also known as the *hungry grass.* Jochen Köser, who has been reading Richard Power's fine novel, wants to know where the name came from.

The *féar gortach* or hungry grass is quaking grass, a mountain grass supposed to have the effect on those who come near it of making them weak and hungry by the power of the fairies. Seumus MacManus in his *Bold Blades of Donegal* says that this bewitched grass was once sat on by some greedy people who ate, and then neglected to leave a bit for Gentle People. Bear this in mind, Jane Crane of Churchill, soon to live in a fairy stronghold in the shadow of Errigal, I'm told.

Another phenomenon know to the old timers was the *seachrán* or *shaughraun.* This was an influence under which the victims, although professing to be perfectly sane and sober, lost themselves on well-known paths. The fairies were blamed again, of course.

In England they had their own kind of seachrán, but they called it *led-will.* I find in *Notes and Queries* of 1895 that 'farmers have been known to walk round and round familiar fields for hours without finding an exit; others to drive for some time, and then to find themselves at their starting point. Persons in this predicament always travel in circles, and the only way of escape is to burn some article of clothing.' '*Led-will* means "led by will", i.e. by a will-o'-

the-wisp, and it is metaphorically applied to one who is in any way puzzled and bewildered by following false lights,' according to a source in the EDD. Ah no. It means led astray, *will* representing Old Norse *villr*, bewildered, erring, astray.

Mary Kinsella of Sutton, but a blow-in from Wicklow, wondered if I've come across the word *libe*, a big slice, a hunk, of bread, for instance. Libe (Irish *leadhb*) means many things in Irish English. In Carlow, it is a rag, a strip of cloth. In Westmeath it means a deep sod. 'He turned up a libe of land"– he ploughed too deeply. In Kilkenny, a libe is a big, slovenly woman; in Mayo, a male half-wit. I have often wondered whether *libe/leadhb* came originally from English. Compare the English dialect word *lipe*, a portion or slice, usually applied to land. Piers Plowman has it: 'The Iewes hauen a lippe of oure byleyue.'

## Earls – Gowlogue – Cutting

One of the interesting Leitrim words my friend the late Gus Martin used was *earls*, which means a pledge, a deposit on a purchase. W.H. Patterson, in his glossary of Antrim and Down words (1880), has the word under *airles*; the EDD has *arles*, taking its cue from Blount's Law Dictionary of 1691 and Bailey's dictionary of 1755. Blount glosses arles as 'argentum Dei (God's silver) – money given in earnest of a bargain'. Bailey has *arles penny*: earnest money given to servants'. Gus Martin's *earls* was an older form. In a manuscript of *c.*1220 we find 'This ure lauerd giueth ham as erles of the eche mede that schal cume thereafter.' The word is in Irish as *éarlais*.

Another of Gus's words was one he spelled *baurna*. I'm puzzled by this one. I found it as well in a collection of Leitrim words made by the Donegal writer , Tadhg Ó Rabhartaigh. He has *báirne*. It means a spectre; it is not in the dictionaries, as far as I know.

From Mary Grace of Kilkenny comes a query about the word *gowlogue*. To her father, she says, the word meant a big drink of whiskey. She knows gowlogue to be the farmers' word for a forked stick used as a protection when cutting furze bushes, and wonders if her father was mistaken. Well, Dinneen has *gabhlóg*, a prop, a support, as well; and *gabhlóg/gowlogue*, a stiff drink, is a figurative use of the word. John Banim has it in *The Croppy*, just an Mr Grace had it: 'Maybe your Reverence 'ud try a gawlogue.' A young friend of mine has just reminded me that the Banim brothers lived in Kilkenny for many years. I'm glad to know that the word survives by the lovely Nore.

John Rochford from Wexford wants to know the origin of the phrase 'There's great *cutting* in him.' The phrase is found all over Ireland, and has not been recorded elsewhere. Cutting is a translation of the Irish *gearradh*. Ó Dónaill's dictionary has 'Fear nach bhfuil gearradh ann – a man who lacks incisiveness.' But where did the Wexford expression 'he stuck it no cuttin', he didn't last long, originate?

Finally, greetings to another Diarmaid Ó Muirithe, from Cúil Aodha, Co. Cork, who informed an RTÉ farming programme recently that he once kept cows but that he rose out of them. *D'éirigh sé astu*, I need hardly tell you.

## Widow Twanky – Tea – Barley – Mess

Monica Heskin from Waterford asks why the Dame in the Aladdin pantomime is called *Widow Twanky*. Well, Twankai, a district in China, was, in Victorian times, famous for its tea, and *twankay* (you'll find the word in Thackeray) became a term for China tea, and then for tea in general. In Victorian pantomime scripts the good lady drank great quantities of tea when she wasn't washing the short and simple flannels of the poor – hence the name.

Tea was, in the days when the great Cobbett was railing about the slavery of the mill children, the luxury of poor women, and their word for a tea-party still survives in Yorkshire and Lancashire – *tutting*. I came across a reference to it recently in Hall's Victorian glossary, which describes it as 'a tea-drinking for women of the lower order, succeeded by stronger potations in the company of the other sex, and ending, as might be expected, in scenes of ribaldry and debauchery'. A Yorkshire friend of mine recently referred to a Macra na Feirme barn dance as 'a great tutting'.

A lady who lives in Crosthwaite Park, Dún Laoghaire, and who desires anonymity, wrote about the term *high tea*. Is it Anglo-Irish, she asks, and why *high*?

Well, *high* is a common superlative. Think of High Court, high commissioner, high command etc. High tea, tea at which meat is served, seems to have originated in England, and we first find it written in 1831, in Kemble's *Recollections of Girlhood*.

Tea, still pronounced *tay* in most of rural Scotland, England and Ireland, is found in some interesting combinations. The meal following a wedding is called a *tay-an'-eatin'* in rural Scotland north of Perth. In rural Lancashire what would nowadays be called a sherry party was once called a *tay-an' rum bagging*, described as a popular festivity among women who club their money together to buy tea, rum, muffins etc. and have a jollification at one of the subscribers' houses. The tea strengthened with rum was called *tay royal*.

By the middle of the last century the Irish middle classes were using tea as a verb: '*He tead with us last night*'; and the author of *Paddiana* (1848) heard '*Will you have tay-tay or coffee-tay?*' from a pretentious female.

I came across a strange term in a tome by Jane Barlow recently. Jane's books are a good source of northern words. The term was *barley bairn*, and it means a child born in wedlock but conceived at least three months before the parents were married. The term is common in Scotland, it seems, and the metaphor lies in the allusion to the time between the sowing and the barley harvest. *Barley crop*, my Yorkshire mine of information on north of England words tells me, is a term used by catty people who count months after a wedding. 'So Maggie's gotten a barley-crop then, the hussy.'

'Does *mess*, as in making a mess of something, and *mess* in officer's mess have a common origin?', asks somebody who signed himself Old Soldier. Yes. Both are from old French *mes*, dish of food from Late Latin *missus*, course at table, from Latin *mittere*, to send forth, to set out. But the mess that survives in 'officer's mess' used to be applied to a group of four people or things. Shakespeare has 'Where are your mess of sons to back you now?' in *Henry VI*. There were four, Edward, George, Richard and Edmund. Latimer in his *Sermons* has 'There lacks a fourth to make up the mess.' Not enough for a tutting.

'Would you consider the ancient Irish word *mias* as the origin of the mess in officer's mess?', Geoffrey Ryan of Santry subsequently asked me. I think I'll stick with what I've already written about this matter, but Mr Ryan makes a good point. *Mias*, from *mes*, from Latin *mensa*, meant a flat board or slab (for supporting food etc.), a table; a tray, platter or dish (as primitive tables were boards laid on trestles, the two meanings are not always distinguishable: my reference is the Royal Irish Academy's Dictionary). I'll stick to my theory that *mess* in *officer's mess* is from Old French, *mes*, dish of food.

## As Pleased as Punch

A reader from Cahir, whose flamboyant signature, reminiscent of those found in Tudor manuscripts and on late Saturday night pub cheques, I cannot make out, wants to know where the terms *as proud as Punch* and *as pleased as Punch* come from.

According to Oxford, the latter phrase was first written by our own Tom Moore in a letter to Lady Donegal dated 1813. Mr Punch has been around since the Restoration. His face, carved in wood and smiling from ear to ear, delighted children young and old. He must have looked proud as well as pleased; I can find no other explanation of the other phrase, used by the late Christy Brown in *Down All the Days*: 'Every man-jack of them sitting there proud as Punch with their sons ...' I am indebted to Nigel Rees and his Bloomsbury *Dictionary of Phrase and Allusion* for the following, a quotation from a letter to Lord Herbert from a Doctor Eyre, dated New Year's Day 1779, and relating to a visit by George III and his Queen to Wilton House: 'The Blue Closet within was for her Majesty's private purposes, where there was a new red velvet Close Stool, and a very handsome China Jordan, which I had the honour to produce from an old collection, and you may be sure, I am proud as Punch that her Majesty condescended to piss in it.'

John Roche from Wexford asks about the Wexford (and Dorset and Somerset) expression, 'She threw me out pack and fardel.' Fardel means baggage, and the word 'comes from the identical Old French, glossed as 'fardeau' by La Curne.

Interestingly, fardel also means the cover of a book in both Wexford and Devon, while the Scots have retained the word with the meaning, load, 'a lot', in such phrases as 'a fardel of lies'.


## Raking – Joog – Rosiner


Here was a time when I thought that Ulster men and women were wild divils compared with us from the sedate south. Northern bookmen were to blame for this. Peadar O'Donnell, Seumus MacManus, Lynn Doyle and about a score more of them went on about their raking exploits in the wee hours, and I suppose I wasn't to blame for thinking that their raking was related to *rake*, a dissipated person, from *rakel*, a variant of *rakehell*, the *rake* bit coming from Old English *raca*, related to Old Norse *raka*, the implement gardeners use, and to the Latin noun *rogus*, a funeral pile, from the Gothic verb *rikan*, to pile up. James Foley from Omagh, writing in the northern journal, *Causeway*, recently, points out that the Ulsterman's *rake* means a friendly visit, so that a *raker* is as far removed from a *rakehell* as one could imagine. Where, he asks me, does this Ulster *rake* originate?

The Scots, the northern English, and, significantly, the Shetland *rake* means to wander, ramble; to stroll about idly; to stay out late at night. I have no doubt that this good word, ignored by the dictionaries because of its dialect status, is from the Old Norse *reika*, to ramble, to stroll.

Dr John Fleetwood tells me that he was recently told by a patient in his Carysfort, Blackrock, clinic that she hadn't a *joog* in her. What, he asks, is a *joog*? She explained that she felt very tired. *Joog* is the Irish *diúg*, a drop. The verb *diúg* means to drain, to drink to the dregs. The lady was born in Dublin. Her word is Dublin Irish.

Dan Swift from Rathfarnham wrote to ask about the word *rosiner*, a stiff drop of the crathur. Well, you won't find this in the dictionaries either, but the EDD is helpful.

The word is indeed related to the *rosin* used by fiddlers, as Mr Swift suspects. In Lancashire, a *rosin* was a jocular term for a drink bought for a musician. In Lincolnshire, 'to rosin 'er up' meant to ply a lady with drink so as to get her warmed up to sing. Oh, yes. In Hampshire, to be *rosined* means to be plastered. The word is found from Northumberland to the southern shires; *rosiner* is found all over Ireland. All from Old French *resine*, from Latin *resina*, from *Greek rhetine*, resin from a pine.

## Scrocky – Slather

Dr James Clarke of Rathcoole recently sent me the word *scrocky*, meaning flaky. An 80-year-old patient complained of having scrocky skin.

Scrocky is from the Irish *scrothach*, a variant of *scrathach*, which means flaky, according to the great 19th-century scholar, John O'Donovan. The noun is *scroth*, or *scraith*, scurf.

Mrs Camilla Raab of Hogarth Hill, London, had the privilege of working with the great Eric Partridge once upon a time. Now she has honoured me by asking me about a few beauties, the first of which is *slather*.

She knows *slather* from the phrase *open slather*, meaning *carte blanche*. It is, she tells me, also used as a verb, to apply a dollop of cream or paste to a cake or to wallpaper.

As to *slather* in *open slather*, what we have here is an English North Country word meaning a downpour, or the flash flood that follows it. A Yorkshire friend of mine tells me that open slather is, literally, unhindered rain or floodwater; the figurative meaning is obvious.

*Slather* is also used in Yorkshire for thin, liquid mud. It may be found elsewhere in England but I haven't come across it in the dialect dictionaries that sprang up like mushrooms in the late 19th century. Confectioners and decorators use it figuratively both as a noun and as a verb.

The word is of Germanic origin, probably imitative. Compare the East Frisian *sladdern*, to rain noisily, to pee in the same fashion.

## Ho – Tally Ho – Snake

I'm sure you know that William Barnes, the Dorsetshire dialect poet, was the man who edited the glossary compiled by the Quaker farmer, Jacob Poole, in south-east Wexford towards the end of the 18th century.

The word *ho*, trouble, worry, is not in Poole, but Barnes has it in one of his poems, and from another Dorset source we have 'In happy days when I were young, an' had noo ho.'

Imagine my surprise when I was told in a letter from Eileen Rossiter, writing from Guildford, that 'ho' was one of her Arklow grandmother's words. 'I haven't a ho in the world,' she'd reply when one enquired about her health.

I've never come across this word in Ireland before. In the south of England they have it as a verb as well, meaning to long for, also to care. 'I cannot understand Farmer Boldwood being such a fool at this time of life as to ho and hanker after thik woman,' wrote Thomas Hardy in *Far from the Madding Crowd*.

Our friend Barnes has 'A don't know an' A don't ho' in his *Dorset Glossary* of 1863. The EDD tells me that it's *oh* in Somerset. Pregnant women are said to oh for things: 'They auvis zaid how his mother oh'd vor strawberries, late in the fall.' The word is from Old English *hogu*, anxiety, care.

A trailing thread below a hemline was a *tallywagger* in Mrs Raab's Limerick mother's English. *Tally* is related to *tail*. Both words come from Old English *taegl*. The EDD has *tallywag* from Cheshire. There it means *membrum virile*.

Incidentally, I think that all the major dictionaries are wrong in their guess as to the origin of the fox-hunting cry, *tally ho!* Perhaps from the 18th-century French hunting cry *taillaut*, they say, every one of them. Poppycock! It's from the good English country word *tally*, tail, fox's brush & *ho*, an old Norse exclamation used to attract attention (Shakespeare and Bertie Wooster have it in *What ho!*). *Tally ho!* is what the huntsman shouts when he first sights the fox. What would them Oxford tallywags know about huntin' anyway?

'I'm sure you've often heard Irish people say things like, "I caught him snaking around my room." To settle an argument, could you please tell me whether this *snake* is related to the much maligned reptile, or is it an Irish mispronunciation of *sneak?*' James Hennebry of Waterford asks.

I'd prefer to call *snake* a dialect word in its own right, as old as *sneak* if not older, and it is found all over Britain. Burns has 'While he, wi' hingin' lips an' snakin', Held up his head' in *Holy Willie's Prayer*, while Scott's pal, Hogg, the shepherd poet, speaks of 'snaikin aboot i' the dark'.

D.H. Lawrence, too, was fond of the word. Its origin? Old English *snikan*, to creep, crawl; Old Norse *snijka*.

But isn't snaking what a snake does? Indeed; but snake comes from Old English *snaca*, Old Norse *snakr*, related to Old High German *snahhan*, to crawl, and also, my dears, to the Irish *snámhaim*, I crawl.

## Binting – Dekko – Naughty – Lich

John Creedon is from Cork and he sent me some of his late father's words and phrases. The old man was a soldier who saw action in the Great War; his son asks about the origin of some of the words he remembers from him.

'I see you're all dressed up. Binting again?' Binting, courting. Arabic *bint*, a girl. I notice that Sheik Mohammed has *bint* as a suffix in some of his fillies' names.

'She's a *barjee* in the Victoria.' The Hindi is *bawarchi*, a cook. 'His *bundock* is the soldier's only friend.' The Swahili is *bunduki*, a rifle.

A *dekko*, a look, as in 'Give us a dekko at the paper' is still heard in many places. The Hindi is *dekhna*, to see; the imperative is *dekho*, look! see!

That pleasant-sounding word *naughty,* nowadays used as a word of mock censure, is the subject of a letter from Joyce Willis of Lichfield, formerly of Sutton. What troubles Joyce is that in some rural areas around her English home, naughty means something a little different. For example, people fed up to the teeth with a local politician might say, 'He's a naughty bugger and should be got rid of.' Naughty here means good-for-nothing.

Naughty has an interesting history. It comes from Old English, *nawiht,* from *na,* no and *wiht,* thing, and early in its history it meant useless. To think that this original meaning still survives! The Bible of Shakespeare's time has, from Jeremiah, 'The other basket had very naughty figs,' and Shakespeare's naughty in 'a good deed in a naughty world' also meant corrupt.

But let's see what the great Dr Johnson from Lichfield had to say about the word. 'Naughty: adj. Bad, wicked corrupt. It is now seldom used but in ludicrous censure.' I feel certain that the old curmudgeon would be happy to know that the older meaning survives still close to his home.

Lichfield itself is an interesting placename. It comes from Old English *lic,* a corpse. So Johnson's town grew up around a graveyard. The *lichgate* in a cemetery was where the bier was put down to allow the mourners to catch up. The owl is known in places as *lichowl,* a bird of ill omen to some of the great names of literature, Pliny, Ovid and Shakespeare among them; whereas in my part of the world to see the owl is a foretoken of good luck. In Wexford Athena's wise old bird still rules OK.

## Japped – Scousing – Scoot

'Or some new white flower japped with crimson' is a line from Seamus Heaney's first poem in *Station Island*. A reader from Ravensdale, Dundalk, asks about the word *japped,* which means splashed.

*Jap* is an import from Scotland, where it is also found as *jaup,* *jawp* and *jalp.* It is found as *jop, jope* and *jowp* in northern England. Heaney's *jap* is common in the Shetlands, in Fife and Edinburgh. 'Like swallin' waves on rough shores jappin', wrote a minor poet called Tennant in 1827. The same poet has *japper*, a broken wave: 'Beside the shore Whairon the' Aegean's jappers roar.' Kelly, in his marvellous *Scottish Proverbs* of 1721 has, ride fair an jaap nane'. In Cumberland they have the noun, plural, *jopins*, anything spilled. The Scots phrase, 'to jawp the water' means to spend time on any business without the least prospect of success.

Old Phil Wall of Carne, Co. Wexford, long gone from us, alas, had jap as a noun, the broken wave flung skywards when it hits the bow of a ship. This is what Burns had in mind when he wrote in *The Brigs of Ayr*, 'Dash the gumlie jaups up to the pouring skies.' *Gumlie* means thick, muddy; gloomy. *Japped*, I think, is onomatopoeic.


Christine O'Connor, of Portstewart, Co. Derry, wrote to tell me that her mother, now in her 83rd year, remembers the regular use of *sconsing* both in her native Donegal and in Derry. It meant teasing, taking a hand. The EDD has it as to joke, chaff, ridicule and quotes various sources from Antrim, Down and Donegal, including 'the kissin' an' jokin' and sconcin' went round'. I don't know the origin of this sconce, I'm sorry to say.


I do know where the word *scoot* comes from. A.J. Hewitt from Dunmurray asks about it. It is a term of the utmost contempt applied to both men and women, he tells me. Another Scots import, I'd say. The poet Leighton, obviously in foul mood in 1869, wrote that a clergyman of his acquaintance, 'A learned pious yet unworthy scoot, Neglects a sacred trust to catch a troot.' Another Scots source told the EDD that 'scoot is a term of the greatest contumely, applied to a woman. A Celt or Highlander can hardly receive greater disgrace than to be thus denominated.' The EDD asks us to compare the Swedish dialect *skjut*, also *skut*, a horse; also a wanton man.

'But I'm for tacklin' Sarah Ann No matter if the snow Is everywhere sheebowin' When the morra comes I'll go.' So wrote W.H. Marshall, and Ruth Bell, a lady from his country up north, wants to know the origin of *sheebow*, a blizzard to you and me.

It's from Irish, *síobadh*, usually found in the compound *síobadh, sneachta*, a blow, or blizzard of snow.

A query from a man who lives a bit to the east of Tyrone, in Lifford, Co. Donegal. 'In my young days, we used to call small potatoes sciddins,' he writes, and wonders if *sciddins* is a Scots importation.

No, the origin of that word is the Irish *scidín*, or its variant *sceidín*. Sciddin is common in the works of Donegal writers. Seumus MacManus, in *The Bend of the Road* has 'He happened to throw up five or six sciadins [*sic*] of praties in the mud.' Patrick MacGill in *Glenmornan* refers to 'scaddan and skiddins', *scaddans* being the Irish *scadáin*, herrings. But as to the Irish scidín or sceidín', Ó Dónaill, another Donegalman, glosses this as 'Small spot, speck, driblet; small thing; small potatoes. Sceidín also means, he says, a little appendage; a scut, a boy's penis.

In the Rosses 'sciddin' has another meaning – a trifle, a worthless present. 'Will you look at the skiddin he bought me for Christmas,' said a singularly unimpressed young lady from near Dungloe as she displayed a ring of dubious quality to a friend. Scidín's the diminutive of *scead*, but where does that come from? Dinneen asks us to consider the Latin, *schedium*, a thing made in a hurry. Fair enough as far as her ladyship's ring is concerned, whatever about spuds, scuts, driblets and small penises.

Mary Power from Waterford wrote to mention an expression of her mother's: 'That fellow is only a *gown soura*.' *Gamhain samhraidh*, a summer calf, reared soft, as they say, on an abundance of milk. A milksop, in other words.

'I was reminded the other night of a very common expression,' writes Michael Brady, a student from Cavan who has pitched his tent in Clontarf. 'I was walking down Dorset Street when I heard a lady who was peering through the window of a public house exclaim: "There he is, the bastard. I'll brain the bowsio when I'll get me hands on him."' *To brain*: 'Does this simply mean that the good lady meant to damage her beloved's cerebrum, assuming that he possessed one?', he asks.

That's all it means, but it is interesting in that it has been around for a long time. Shakespeare has it in *Henry IV*, part 1: 'Zounds, an I were now by this rascal I could brain him with his lady's fan,' said Hotspur getting hot under the collar. But Mr B.'s letter reminded me of another Shakespearian to brain, meaning to understand, comprehend, figure out. I have heard this verb once or twice in Co. Wicklow. 'Brain it out for yourself, if you can,' said a man from Glenealy direction to me recently, referring to recent mysterious financial transactions.

The only reference to it in the EDD cites a Suffolk source; but the same EDD is almost useless when it comes to the dialect words of Ireland, apart from Wexford's southern baronies and some of the counties of Ulster. But, as I say, Shakespeare has it, in *Cymbeline*. ''Tis still a dream, or else such stuff as madmen tongue and brain not.' Is this *brain* of Shakespeare's to be found in other parts of Ireland? I'd like to know.

'*Bully man!* is a term of endearment in Co. Donegal, usually addressed to a youngster,' Anne Gillespie wrote to tell me. As if I didn't know, being married to a Donegal woman. They have it in Connacht as well, by the way, and in other northern counties besides Donegal. They have *bullaí fir!* in the Gaeltacht areas, and Anne implies that the English expression was borrowed from the Irish.

Hold hard there, girl. It was in English long before the Gaeltacht people got to know of it. Your man from Stratford has it in that naughty play, *A Midsummer Night's Dream*, when Flute, the bellows-mender, exclaims, 'O sweet bully Bottom!'

But the English in their turn borrowed the word from the Middle Dutch *boele,* sweetheart.

Related to the other bully, a persecutor of weaker people? Yes, through a common enough process that changed the Dutch word for sweetheart into something that meant its antithesis. Sin mar a bhíonn.

## Mealy-mouthed – Huffle – Jook

'Where does the expression *mealy mouthed* originate?', asks John Barry from Blackrock in Cork. A darlin' question, John, and one that has caused divisions among the etymologists. Some are still convinced that *mealy* is connected with the *mel*-root that we find in the Greek and Latin for honey, and, of course, in the Irish *mil.* But the general consensus nowadays is that this is a false etymology, and that the source is *meal,* grain ground to a powder, whose ultimate *origin* is Latin *molere,* to grind. All related, of course, to Latin *mola, molina*; whence English *mill,* French *moulin,* and Irish *muileann.*

A query about the word *huffle,* heard in the Arklow of his youth by a reader who wants to be anonymous. It was used, he says, by old seafaring men of wind blowing in sudden, fierce gusts. William Barnes, the dialect poet of Dorset, has this: 'Where sharp-leaved ash's heads did twist in hufflen wind, and driften mist.' An old word, this. Dublin's Richard Stanyhurst has it in his *Aeneis* in 1583: 'To swage seas surging, or raise by blusterus huffling.' Of imitative origin, like *puff.*

Ann Gallagher, who hails from Churchill in Co. Donegal, asks about the verb *jook,* to evade, to dodge something or somebody. Also spelled *jouk* and *juke,* it is common all over the north. Patterson in his glossary of Down and Antrim words has the aphorism 'Juke and let a jaw flee': take no notice of angry words; stoop and let it pass over you. Seumus MacManus has 'He went jookin' an' creepin' roun' be the ditches.' Hence they have *jookhalter,* one who narrowly escaped being hanged, and *jook-the-beetle,* lumps in stirabout or colcannon. *To jook* also means to swindle, and the *Ballymena Observer* of 1890 also gives us *jookery* and *jook-packery*, doubledealing.

Jook is very common in Scotland, where a jooking stream meanders, and a jooking light flickers. Its origin? You may have guessed it. It is related to the verb *duck*. Germanic. Compare Old High German *tuthan*, to dive; Middle Dutch *duken*.


## *Holyawn —Rabbie Burns*

A few interesting letters about the Wexford word *holyawn*, a brat, a young hooligan, all of them disagreeing with my guess regarding its etymology. I wrote that I suspected that the word's origin was the Irish *teolán*, a little thief. One reader, Martin O'Brien from Limerick, asks me to consider *uallán*, 'a lighthearted skittish person' according to Ó Dónail's dictionary. Patrick Fennessy, of Gurrane, Ballyhea, Charleville, suggests *áilleán*, 'a toy, a trinket, a doll; a dressed up, useless person', according to Ó Dónail. Not enough of the hooligan element in these for me. Máire Nic Mhaoláin suggests that the word may be related to the northern and Scottish, *hallion*. Mícheál Ó Loingsigh of Wicklow town wrote: 'I often heard my Enniscorthy mother refer to people she didn't like very much as *Uhlans*. She explained to me that Wexford people had reason to despise these people, because of the atrocities committed by them in 1798.' (The Uhlans were originally lancers in the Polish Army. By the time the Wexfordmen set the heather blazing, the German heavy cavalry was know by this name.) Were these the original holyawns? No, I'm afraid. The German and Polish word comes, by the way, from the Turkish *oglan*, a young man, a soldier.


As all the world knows, Robert Burns left us two hundred years ago. A correspondent from Athy asks me to recommend a reasonably-priced Burns anthology that contains a glossary. She has a little trouble with the great poet from Ayrshire, she tells me, and no wonder. Try *Rhymer Rab*, edited by Alan Bold, published by Black Swan at around £8. Brendan Adams tried out these words of Burns on people who lived north of Ballymena, and found that most of them posed no problem. Just how many of these could *you* explain, southern reader?

*Acquesh*: between. *Aiblins*: maybe. *Asklent*: askew. *Awnie*: bearded. *Biggin*: cottage. *Bitchifyed*: drunk. *Blate*: shy. *Blue boram*: pox. *Chapman*: pedlar. *Brose*: oatmeal mixed with boiling water. *Butter'd my brose*: satisfied me sexually. *Damn'd haet*: damn all. *Creeshie*: filthy. *Donsie*: restive, bad-tempered. *Eldricht*: haunted. *Forfochten*: exhausted. *Havins*: manners. *Houghmagandie*: fornication. *Lintie*: linnet. *Mowe*: copulate. *Pawkie*: sly, cunning. *Luntin*: smoking. *Crack*: conversation.

## Mortal Eegit – Merdle – Twit

A man from Mullingar writes to ask whether the adjective *mortal*, used as an intensitive to signify great, extreme, serious, fine, grand, is confined to the midlands. 'I feel like a mortal eegit to ask the queskin,' he says.

Mortal used in this sense is found all over the place, and it is just as common in Scotland, England and America as it is here. How old it is I don't know. I can trace it no further back than the 18th century. Grose, in his famous *Classical Dictionary of the Vulgar of Tongue* has, 'He's a mortal good doctor.' A contemporary of Rab Burns has 'Aye, she was mortal wild.'

An equally interesting mortal is found in Scotland, and I've often wondered if it has found its way to the north of Ireland. It means fluthered, dead drunk. 'He was often carried home in a hand-barrow, just mortal' was reported from Galloway; as was 'The Pilgrim was drunk when he went oot, an' he came back mortal.'

Hence *mortallacious* and *mortallious*, both confined to the Newcastle district of England, it would seem, and meaning absolutely plastered. The words, I'm reliably informed, are still used by the fuzz in that city's courts, and understood by the ladies and gentlemen on the Bench.

Thanks to Carol Sharpe, late of Coleraine, for the word *merdle*, 'a big family of wains', she says. This word came from Scotland, and is of French origin. The great Cotgrave gives us the answer. Those early 17th-century lexicographers didn't mince their words, and our friend says that the original *merdaille* was, 'a crew of shitten knaves or filthy scowndrels, of stinking fellows'.

The word *twit*, idiot, is bothering Mary Carr from Cork. The great dicionaries can trace it no further back than the 19th century, and all say that it's related to the verb *twit*, to tease, traceable to Old High German *wizan*, to punish. Ah, so.

But twit was also a 19th-century weaving term, anything entangled; that which gave resisting power to the thread. The twit was the greatest nuisance encountered in weaving. A Lancashire and Yorkshire word, *twit* was transferred to the human equivalent, the mortal eegits of the mill towns. That much is incontestable. With great humility I offer it as the answer to Mrs Carr's question.

## Matters Medical

Dr James Clarke, who practises medicine in Rathcoole, Co. Dublin, recently heard a very interesting and rare word used by an elderly patient. The word as the good man wrote it down was *comer;* the patient had complained half-seriously that the tablets he had given her didn't take a comer out of the pain.

This word, which means inconvenience, trouble, is related to *encumbrance*, and is found as *cummer, comer, cumber* and *cummar* in Scotland, England and the north of this country. It is ancient. Dunbar has 'Sic hunger, sic cummer within this land was nevir hard nor sene,' in *Devorit with dreme,* written about 1510; and Tindale's translation of St Luke, written in 1526, has 'Martha was combred about moche servynge.' The word is also used in England's North Country as a verb meaning to oppress, to trouble. A Yorkshire patient might say, 'I'm comered with pain.'

The word, in all its manifestations, is from Old French *encombrer*, to encumber.

Frans Frison of Killiney has subsequently pointed out that Dutch has *kommer*, distress, trouble, sorrow, and that German has *Kummer*, sorrow, grief, trouble. He speculates that *comer* is Germanic in origin, and that I may be wrong in tracing it to France.

There seems to be near unanimity among lexicographers that *cummer/kummer/comer* etc. are from the French word. The excellent American *World Book Dictionary*, however, says that *encombrer* itself may be Germanic in origin. Collins says that it is from the Late Latin *cumbrus*, a word of uncertain origin. Oxford says that the date, form and sense are all consistent with its being either a derivative or a shortening of *encombrer*, but that the sense trouble, distress, strikingly coincides with Middle High German *kummer* (from 1200) not to mention the modern word.

It seems to me that the answer to our problems lies in *cumbrus* and its mysterious origin. Odds on it's Germanic.

Let's stay with matters medical. Margaret Whitty, born in Wexford, wrote to tell me that her grandmother used a word she has never heard since the old lady died some ten years ago. The word is *bleeze*, and Margeret asks if it is used still anywhere. Old Mrs W. was very worried about the deleterious effects of the mini-skirt on the bleeze, it seems. Bleeze means bladder.

What an old word this is. I've never heard it, but if you know anything at all about the origins of Wexford English you won't be surprised that I found it in a dictionary of the Pembrokeshire dialect, which spells it *bleaze*, by the way, not that that matters. Bleeze represents the Old English *blaese*, a bladder; Middle High German *blase* and Old High German *blasa*.

And finally, Máire Nic Mhaoláin tells me that *coup*, to turn upside down, is often *cope* in east Co. Down. But, she points out, many people in that part of the world would never use the fashionable 'I just can't cope, doctor.' To cope also means to evacuate the bowels, where the mountains of Mourne sweep down to the sea.

# Yewk — Gype — Lig — Sloother — Lift

The word *yewk*, to itch, is one that hasn't, as far as I know, travelled further south than Cavan and Monaghan. It seems to be a Scots import; in that language it has a long pedigree. The word is also found as a noun, meaning the itch, and hence we get *yewkiness*. An old Scots proverb says 'Love is a yewkiness of the heart that the hand canna claw.' The word was recorded by Patterson, Hume and others in Antrim and Down a hundred years ago. It is of Germanic origin. You'll find *jucken* in Middle High German, *joken* in Middle Low German; and the Dutch have *jeuken*, to itch. I thank Mary MacGowan for sending the word my way from Monaghan.

Seán Ó Donnagáin, a man of Offaly stock who now lives in Dublin, sent me a story about a group of Tyrone labourers who called a young fellow who was employed to run errands and make tea the *gype*. The English ganger one day asked the senior workman what a gype was, and the answer he got was, 'It's halfway between a lig and a shloother.' Most enlightening.

Well now, *gype* is found in the north of this country and in Scotland. As a verb it means to stare foolishly; to act as a fool. As a noun it means a fool, a lout; an awkward, stupid fellow. These definitions are the EDD's. From Old Norse *geip*, nonsense.

What about a *lig*? This is Scots, too. It is a doublet of *lag*. A *lig*, sometimes *ligger*, is one who stays in bed all day; a useless lazy person; one who is habitually late. Both *lig* and *lag* are of unknown origin; *lig* was used in Scots when Shakespeare referred to 'the lag end of my life'.

As for *shloother*, I would ask you to compare the Irish *sluaiste*, a layabout, and the Scots Gaelic *sluaisteach*, of shuffling gait.

In the Cooley peninsula people once used the expression 'He'd charm the larks out of the lift.' It was often applied to young men more successful than most in the art of seduction. So a bashful 'Ruth, from Dundalk' tells me. No shloothers, these Cooleymen.

This *lift* is Scandinavian in origin, related to Old Norse *lypta*, and Old English *lyft*, sky. Interestingly, the EDD gives 'to suck the laverocks (larks) out of the lift' from Scotland. Compare the Modern German *Luft,* air, the Irish *lochta,* loft, and indeed the Modern English *loft, aloft* and *lofty.*

'It must be a while since your column received correspondence from Angola,' writes Stephen Jackson, Director of Trócaire in that far-off land. Stephen's query is about the words *lig, ligging* and *ligger.* I'll let the man speak for himself: 'The words were in use not just in Trinity College, Dublin, while I was there (less than ten years ago) but across the Irish university circuit, particularly in debating circles. A lig was a freebie, a reception with free booze, which could be gate-crashed. Ligging was the activity of gate-crashing, and a ligger was an inveterate crasher. To become a ligger involved paying ten quid to buy a monkey suit from a charity shop, the automatic ticket to most ligs being a black tie. I think we believed lig to be a borrowing from Irish, in the sense of *lig do scíth.* The term seemed to us to have some antiquity.'

Lig, ligger and ligging are no older than the 1960s, Stephen, and they were first recorded in the journals *Twentieth Century* and *Melody Maker.* Undoubtedly they reached Trinity through the popular music scene, and, according to a young friend of mine who has recently been commenced there, they are still in use. *Lig* is an obsolete word for *lie,* a fib, from Old English *lyge.*

## Cowl – Arklooker – Slush

Mr Kevin Hannan, President of the Old Limerick Society, writes to ask about the origin of the word *cowls.* It was, he says, 'used to describe the site of a building long since demolished, and almost all the fabric taken away.'

This is the Irish *cabhail,* which means, among other things that include the body, a trunk, the hold of a ship, a camisole, the bare walls of a house, according to Father Dinneen; a ruin according to Ó Dónaill.

Mr Séamus Mohan of Rathdowney, Co. Laois, sent me a parcel of interesting words recently. One is *arklooker.* 'When we walked to our rural school in the late 1950s we kept an eye out for these animals, lizards I think, which, we believed, could jump into our mouths and thence to our stomachs.' This word is from the Irish *earc iuachra*, lizard, newt, eft, of the *luachair* or rushes.

Thanks to correspondents I now have twelve Anglo-Irish names for the little green lizard, *earc luachra*. Rev. Canon Henry V. Boake, who lives in Co. Carlow, writes: I remember hearing it pronounced *Dark Luker* about 75 years ago, and as far as I remember I haven't heard of the creatures since. More is the pity: I have a very soft spot for them, as they almost certainly saved my life.' He goes on to explain.

'When I was about five or six I went to stay with an aunt who lived on a farm near Bagenalstown. I wasn't in her house very long when she warned me that on no account was I to go near water barrels, or water tanks, or ponds, or wells. They were full of Dark Lukers and they would immediately jump down my throat. However, if by any chance I did get a Dark Luker down my throat, there was a cure. I would have to stand with my mouth open over a churn of buttermilk until the Luker was sufficiently enticed by the smell of the fresh buttermilk to come up and slip into the churn. This might take all day or longer. I didn't fancy having this cure, so I obeyed my aunt and lived happily ever afterwards.'

Recent references in the papers to *slush funds* allegedly acquired or used by friends of Mr Robert Dole prompted Nancy Stone of Long Island, on a prolonged holiday here, to enquire about the origin of the phrase.

Let's take *slush* first. This slang sailors' word originally meant the refuse, fat or grease obtained from meat boiled on board ship. In 1757 a landlubber, writing about conditions aboard His Majesty's ships, referred to 'tars whose stomachs are not very squeamish, and who can bear to paddle their fingers in stinking slush'. This slush was the perquisite of the ship's cook. But the goo was often stolen by the sailors, who used it to grease masts to make sail-hoisting easier. The cook sold the slush ashore to candle-makers, to fish-and-chip shops, and also to harness makers who used it to preserve leather.

The term *slush fund*, however, seems to have originated in the

US navy. In 1839 it was explained in a book called *Evils and Abuses in the Naval and Merchant Service*. Its author wrote: 'The sailors in the Navy are allowed salt beef ... From this provision, when cooked, nearly all the fat boils off. This is carefully skimmed and put into empty beef or pork barrels, and sold, and the money so received is called the slush fund.'

The term became associated with politicians by the 1800s. The *Congressional Record* has an entry that goes: 'Cleveland was not elected in 1888 because of Pious John Wannamaker and his $400,000 campaign slush funds.'

## Moss House – Sally Lunn

'Oh were I at the moss house where the birds do increase, At the foot of Mount Leinster or some silent place, By the streams of Bunclody, where all pleasures do meet, And all I would ask is one kiss from you, sweet.'

Ann Byrne wrote to me recently from Melbourne about the lovely song. She wants to know what a moss house is. She can thank the Wexford historian Rory Murphy and a sweet Bunclody lady, Sarah O'Hara, for answering a question that has been bothering myself for years. Sarah tells me that the moss house in question was made in the last century by Lady Lucy Maxwell on the Carrigduff side of the Slaney at Bunclody. It was made from actual growing trees which were bent over and intertwined to form a beautiful living summerhouse. Several low, shrub-like trees decorated the floor, which was carpeted with thick, soft moss. Hence the name.

Does the beautiful moss-house still exist, the arbour where the young man, wounded in love, wanted to die on the bosom of his beloved? Alas, no. Vandalism has seen to that.

Who were they anyway, the young lovers? She, I once heard, was one of the Maxwells. Maybe. 'It is why my love slights me, as you may understand, That she has a freehold and I have no land; She has great store of riches and a large sum of gold. And everything fitting a house to uphold.'

And who was *he*? Does anybody know? Mary Byrne and I would love to.

[93]

Eddie Wymberry from Waterford has sent me an engaging little book of reminiscences called *Spring Gardens*, and it includes a collection of words. I see that they ate *Sally Lunns* in Waterford as well as *blahs*.

The lady who gave her name to this tea-cake was an 18th-century Bath pastry cook. She had a portable oven from which she sold the buns for three pence a dozen. She was lovely, was our Sally, and one of her regular customers was a Major Ronald Drew (I'm serious), who published a poem about her cakes in the *Bath Chronicle* in 1796: 'Take thou of luscious wholesome cream What the full pint contains, Warm as the native blood which flows In youthful virgins' veins.' It goes on in that vein. Some poet, some poem: but if you want his recipe I'll send it to you.

## Old Fogy –Dowser

The phrase *old fogy* is bothering a man from Clonmel who describes himself as one. 'Of unknown origin' is all his dictionary has to offer about the noun, and I am asked if I can do any better than that.

Oxford guesses that it may be related to the 18th-century slang word *fogram*, an old-fashioned, antiquated person, and admits that the origin of the slang word itself is unknown. I personally think that *fogy* is related to the Scots word *foggie* (same pronunciation), from Scots *fog*. This particular fog is Scandinavian in origin, and has survived in Norwegian as *fogg*. It means weak scattered grass that grows in a meadow. Hence, figuratively, an old person.

An early occurrence of *fog* is found in the Anglo-Latin *fogagium*, the privilege of pasturing cattle on *fog*. There is a small yellow bee, called in Scotland a *foggie bummer* and a *foggie bee*, so named from its rough appearance, as if covered with moss, according to the EDD.

At any rate, the word *fogy* became common in the last century. In England and Scotland it came to mean an invalid soldier, and in Ireland specifically a pensioner of the Royal Hospital in Kilmainham. Lover had 'He was just like a cut-down fogy' as far back as 1848, in his *Legends*. And that's all this old fogy can offer on the word.

Dublin taxi men have given me many interesting words over the years, and only last week a nice man who lives in Tallaght, in thanking me for my usual generous tip, used the word *dowser*, a word I never heard before. It is alive and well in England, it seems, where, in the West Country, it means a lollipop, and, in London town, a fee, a gratuity. The word is from French *douceur*, sweetness; also a tip. Mayhew recorded the interesting compound *douceur-man* in his *Prisons of London* (1862); 'Douceur-men, who cheat by pretending to get government situations, or provide servants with places, or to tell persons of something to their advantage.'

The adjective *douce* is still to be heard in Donegal. I've hear it pronounced *doose*. It means kind, pleasant, jolly. The word is common in Scotland as well. Burns wrote of 'Ye doose folk I've borne aboon the broo' in *The Brigs of Ayr*. From the French *douse*, sweet, pleasant, this.


## Groping in Groops — Red-up

James Baxter, a Cavan man now living in Dublin, wrote to me to ask where the word *groop* — a trench in a byre into which cow dung was shovelled — came from. The same day's post brought a letter from a lady who lives near The Harrow in Co. Wexford, whose name I cannot reveal.

She asks about the word *gripe*, a word she has been amused by ever since a handsome gentleman asked her out of a dance in that part of the world 50 years ago with the enticingly romantic promise of bein' fairly sure, like, that he could find them a dry gripe to go into for an oul' hoult.

A gripe is a dike, a northern sheugh. And, gentle readers, she tells me that she went and that she has never regretted it. A year or two later, she married him.

Well now, *groop* and *gripe* are cousins, so to speak. Gripe is found all over Ireland, and is just as common in England, where it is also found as *grip*, *grape*, *greape*, and *greep*. Tennyson, in one of his mistaken incursions into dialect verse, has 'An 'e ligs on 's back i' the greep.' Scotland and Orkney also have this word in one form or another.

*Groop* is very popular in Scotland, where it is known only in Mr Reilly's sense of a channel in the floor of a cowhouse. Both words are from Old English *greop*, a trench. The English word is cognate with Middle Low German *grope*, Middle Dutch *greppe*, and the more modern *greop*, a trench.

I'm not sure if medieval Germans groped in gropes, but the word that means to feel with the hands, to examine, according to the saints of Oxford, is itself an old word. It is in Old English as *grapian*, cognate with Old Norse *greipa*, to snatch, grab. That's enough of sex for one day.

Madge McQuaid, of Betty Glen, Raheny, asks me the origin of *to red up*, to tidy. This seems to be confined to the northern part of Ireland. Carleton has 'Tom's barn that was red up for us.' But *red(d)* is also found in Scotland and in northern England. By inversion, the phrase *a fine red-up* is still used in Yorkshire, I'm told, to indicate a sense of disorder. This *red* is from Old English *(ge)raeddan*, to arrange, direct, provide for.

## Toilet – Splurt – Aizel

To my great surprise I heard a Carlow woman refer recently to a dressing-table as a *toilet*. I thought that this meaning had been dead since Pope's day. He, you may remember, used it of Belinda: 'And now, unveiled, the toilet stands displayed, Each silver Vase in mystic order laid.' Pope also knew 'toilet', as the process of making up, which is what he had in mind when he wrote, 'The long labours of the toilet cease', a sentence which might be misunderstood nowadays, even between Borris and Mount Leinster.

A French import, *toilette* was in its country of origin the diminutive of *toile*, a hunting net, a cloth, a web. It came from Latin *tela*, a web. In its new home it was at first a cloth used for wrapping up clothes. Then it became a towel placed on the shoulders of a client by a barber or around a wound by a surgeon. Then it became a linen cloth covering a dressing table, and, as I've said, afterwards the table itself. The Americans first designated a lavatory a toilet; the Europeans in turn re-imported this word to replace older words now considered vulgar.

D.M. MacDermott from Elphin, Co. Roscommon, tells me he and his neighbours have been searching in vain in their dictionaries for the local word *splurt*. This dialect word which means 'a spurt; a splutter, explosion; a sudden start or movement', was, according to the EDD, who thus defined it, obsolete by 1900. Ah no. It is quite common here in the south. A neighbour's child who had poured a half bottle of ketchup over her dress explained that it splurted out. Of unknown origin, like its cousin, *spurt*, I'm sorry to say.

M. Hegarty from Fanad, Co. Donegal, asks about the origin of *aizel*, a red coal, an ember.

*Aizel* came to Ulster from Scotland, via Old English *ysle*, a glowing ember. There are variants, *essel*, *easle*, *isel*, *isil*, found in Scotland and south of the English border as far as Essex, where a distinction was made in the old days between the burning relics of wood and straw; as *easles* of straw and *embers* of wood. Burns, in *Halloween*, has 'She notic'd na an aisel brunt Her braw new worset apron.' The Old Norse for an ember was *usli*; I once heard an Antrim man describe Co. Down women as *oozley shelties*. He was speaking of their hot tempers, I think.

A reader from Sutton, Co. Dublin, Margaret Gannon by name, asks if there are any words, apart from *craic*, which annoy me for one reason or another.

Once upon a time a large *browl* (Irish *breall*, an oaf) who had been instructed to put the peasantry in their places, attempted to evict myself and a very distinguished old man from Bennettsbridge by the name of Hubert Butler from a Requiem Mass. The seats we had occupied in the nave were for *dignitaries*, we were told. The dignitaries turned out to be a *sherogany* (a south Wexford word this, a crowd, origin unknown) of politicians, captains of local industry and their wives, clergymen and nuns, professional people excluding teachers and a full back line of strong farmers. The eviction attempt failed. Now, I didn't give a curse about not being classed as a dignitary, but old Hubert, with whom I had corresponded about words but had never previously met, I felt for, though he seemed amused. I have disliked the word dignitary ever since. It came here from Old French *degnité* (the French have since Latinised their spelling to *dignité*), from Latin *dignitas* from *dignus*, worthy. *Dignus* old Hubert and I were not.

*Enthusiast* is another word I'm not fond of. I don't like being classed as one. The word seems to be applied nowadays only to eccentrics, like those interested in Irish. But in times more civilised than ours when a person got very interested in a subject it was thought that a god had taken possession of him. The Greeks had a word for his possession, *enthusiasmos*, from *enthos*, a god within, from *en*, in, and *theos*, god.

There are, of course, those who, in their honesty, would call the enthusiast a *fanatic*. This word had its origins in Roman temples (Latin *fanum*). It was assumed that in the vicinity of temples one might sometimes find people of extreme convictions. Such a person was called *fanaticus*, which gave English *fanatic*, a word the American baseball enthusiasts shorted to *fan*.

I'm in a sardonic mood as I write this, in a mood to laugh with scorn, especially at dignitaries. But it is interesting how that word *sardonic* has evolved. It came to us from French *sardonique*, itself from late Greek *Sardonios*, Sardinian. The natives of that island, the Greeks believed, knew of a plant of which they who ate died laughing. Don't read too many election leaflets. They could have the same effect.


## *Words from* The Shepherd's Calendar

Jonathan Briggs, a young man from Manchester, wrote to me recently about work he is doing in connection with a thesis on John Clare. He sent me a collection of the poet's words, and he asks if these are found outside Clare's north country. Good dialect words, like good folk songs, tend to travel, and for your amusement this morning I give you some words from *The Shepherd's Calendar*. If you've heard any of them anywhere in this country, please let me know. I can place some of them myself, thanks to readers of this column; locations in parenthesis. Here goes:

*Chimble*: to nibble. *Crank*: To sing in a mournful fashion.

Readers may remember this word from a recent column (Waterford). *Crizzle*: to make rough, as water, when it begins to freeze. *Croodle*: to huddle, to cuddle up for protection, or warmth, or for the other reason (Wexford, south Carlow).

*Douse*: to soak or drench in putting out a fire or a light (General, I should think). *Edding*: a headland, grass at the end of a field where the plough is turned (Wexford). *Elting-moulds*: *the* soft ridges of freshly-ploughed land.

*Fret*: to thaw. *Gleg*: to peep (north Co. Dublin). I've heard *gleek* in Tipperary, said to small children. *Higgling*: searching. *Hulk*: a temporary shelter, used by shepherds in the lambing season (Louth). *Jilt*: to throw underhand with a quick and suddenly arrested motion (east Wicklow). *Lare*: resting place: the place animals are accustomed to stay in: a clearing. Not related to lair, according to my Manchester friend. I wonder. *Lob*: to walk heavily (Waterford, Wexford, Tipperary). *Mawl*: to drag along wearily. *Moiling*: working hard, toiling (Kildare). *Pansion*: a large earthenware bowl.

*Pooty*: a snail shell. *Pudgy*: watery, full of puddles. *Rott*: rat (west Cork). *Sawn*: saunter. 'He came sawnin' down the road. *Scutter*: to scuttle, to run along briskly. *Scuttle*: a basket, or a horse's nose-bag. *Sifter*: kitchen shovel, fire shovel. *Sile*: to glide past. *Slive*: to slide, to slip past quickly. *Soodle*: to dawdle, saunter (Donegal, Sligo, Leitrim). *Stulp*: the stump of a tree. *Sturnel*: starling. *Sturt*: to startle, disturb. *Swaily*: shady, cool. *Ted*: to turn new-mown hay. *Toze*: to pluck, to snatch. *Waffle*: to yap, bark. *Younker*: youngster.


## Mulvather, Hurdies and Latherick

In Bram Stoker's story, *Snake's Pass*, set in Mayo and published in 1891, we find the word *mulvather*. It means to confuse, bamboozle, and the EDD informs me that it is not found outside of Ireland. I've never heard the word, but I'm reliably informed it is still to be heard in parts of Donegal and Tyrone.

Stoker has this: 'He was so much mulvathered at the shnake presumin' to stay, after he tould thim all to go, that for a while he didn't think it quare that he could shpake at all.' Samuel Lover has the word in *Legends and Stories of Ireland* (1884): 'For it was only mulvatherin people they were.' He also used the word in the sense of confused with drink, and he suggests that the word also means to act the gom.

Andrew Bell, who lives in the Lagan, not far from Strabane, wants to know the origin of the word *hurdies*, the buttocks.

It seems to be confined to the north and is undoubtedly Scottish in origin. Many northern writers were fond of it: MacGill, Peadar O'Donnell and Seumus MacManus among them.

Simmons has it in his glossary of south Donegal English (1890). Burns has: 'His gawcie tail wi' upward curl Hung owre his hurdies wi' a swirl' in *Twa Dogs*. 'How cou'd ye ca' my hurdies fat,' asked a lesser poet, Ramsay, in 1724.

The EDD has *hurdy-caikle*, 'a pain in the loins commonly felt by reapers, and occasioned by stooping'. The word was in Scots as far back as 1535, when the estimable Lyndesay wrote: 'Of her hurdies scho had na hauld.' Figure that one out.

I don't know what the young Master Brian Byrne of Raheny was up to in his youth when his long-suffering mother used to shout 'I declare to God I'll cut *lethericks* off o' your backside when I'll catch you.'

I've heard this word in south Dublin and in north Wicklow. It is, I feel sure related to the English North Country word, *latherick*, a slice, a rasher of bacon. Origin? I don't know.


## Tom and Jerry – Tisick – Bauchle

I was interested to hear that an American psychologist wants the cartoon characters, Tom and Jerry, banished from the television screens of his nation. Too much attempted mayhem, you see, the sort of thing that leads little people to shoot and bomb later on in life. No mention of amending gun laws in this unco guid's thesis; just let's get rid of the cat and mouse, guys, as the first step on the road to the Model Society.

The original Tom and Jerry were characters in Pierce Egan's *Life in London*, a fascinating book published in 1821 and continued, owing to popular demand, in 1828. From their antics the verb to Tom-and-Jerry, to behave riotously, came into English colloquial speech; the Regency came to be known as Tom-and-Jerry days, as did the reign of that monstrous oaf, Ireland's friend, George the Fourth. A little later in the century Tom-and-Jerry was applied to a shebeen and also to the House of Commons.

Not long ago I heard a man who lives between Glenmore and Mullinavat in south Kilkenny 'speak of a *tisick*'. He knew the cause of the tisick – too many *cigarettes* – and he vowed to give them up. I had heard this word before in his part of the world and had forgotten it. It means a cough. It is another of those wonderful Tudor survivals; Shakespeare has Pandarus complain in *Troilus and Cressida*: 'A whoreson tisick, a whoreson rascally tisick so troubles me.' The word lives on in many other parts of Ireland.

James Sproule, a Derryman who now lives in London, sends me the word *bauchle*, a down-and-out person.

An interesting word this is, and it came from Scotland to the north. Mr Sproule's is a figurative use; *bauchle*, sometimes spelled *bachal* and *bauchel*, is glossed in the dialect dictionaries as a worn-out shoe or boot. The *Ballymena Observer* glossed *bauchle* as an awkward, clumsy person. In Antrim, they also had, or have, to bauchle, to wear shoes out of shape, and to bauchle a person means to jilt him or her, to treat contemptuously. Hence *bauchling*, reproaching, taunting. A tract called *Seal of Cause for the Hammyrmen*, dated 1496, complained that 'the said craft is abusit be vile persones in bachlying of the Hammyrmenis work'. (Ná bí dána. A hammyr-man was a quarryman, a stonecutter.)

*Bauchel* in all its forms. is from Scots Gaelic *bachall*, an old shoe.

## Cap – Dun

Mary Friel from Derry wrote to ask what the origin of the northern verb *cap* is. It means to stop the progress of any object; to catch; to confine, turn or head back an animal.' 'Used most commonly in herding cattle; also to run after for the purpose of stopping,' says a reliable source, Simmons' *Glossary* of 1890. The word hides under *kep* in the dictionaries, where it is described as Scottish. From Burns' country we find in Service's *Notandrums* (1890): 'They can neither milk, muck a byre, card, spin, nor even kep a coo from the corn-rigg.' Hence the Scots word *keppie*, adjective, quick at turning or heading back an animal. Mactaggart's *Encyclopaedia* of 1824 has 'If they were as keppie as catchie they would make gude shepherd's dogs.'

But where did *cap/kep* come from? Oxford says that these are differentiated forms of the verb *keep*, in an obsolete sense, to put oneself in the way of. (Originally *keep* was Old English *cepan*, to observe). It explains that the short vowel of the past tense, *kept*, has been carried into the present and infinitive.

Well now, I'm not so sure about that. What about the Irish and Scots Gaelic *ceap*, to block the path, to stop, catch, confine? Ó Dónaill's dictionary has 'ainmhí a cheapadh', to head off an animal; Donegal footballers talk of 'an liathróid a cheapadh', to catch the ball; and in Middle Irish we find *ceppaid* (*cepp*), confines, restricts. The origin of *ceap* is Latin, *cippus*, a pallisade, a fence made from sharp stakes. So, am I right, and Oxford wrong?

Regarding a recent reference I made to the early Irish word *donn*, brown, inclining to yellow, which gave Old English *dunn* and Old Norse *dunna*, wild duck (from its colour), Mary Kelleher of Douglas, Cork, reminds me of Lebor na hUidre, the Book of the Dun Cow, now in the Royal Irish Academy. This great treasure of Clonmacnoise, the oldest surviving manuscript written entirely in Irish, was written on parchment, so the legend has it, from the hide of St Ciarán's dun cow. In recent times, when the great book was restored, scholars who use the Academy's library were invited to write a limerick. This won the prize: 'Said Ciarán to his cow after Mass, 'You're dun, and you'll get no more grass, For the scholars and scribes Are descending in tribes To write sagas all over your ass.' I've forgotten who wrote it.

## Looderamaun – Playsham

Monica O'Connell from Cork city remembers a phrase of her

west Cork father's and wonders what its origin is. She spells it *risharrig*. Of an awkward sort of a hurler he remarked: 'Look at him going around in a risharrig, falling over himself and getting in everybody's way.' Well, Monica's word is the Irish *rith searraigh*, literally a foal's run, and anybody who has seen a spring foal's gallop around a paddock will know how apt the phrase is. Dinneen defines it as an impetuous rush, a reckless manner, an unsustained effort.

A lady from Clifden has a query about the common word *loodheramaun*, so spelled by Joyce in *Ulysses*. (He has it as *luderman* in *Finnegans Wake*.) In *Ulysses* he wrote, 'there was an old one with a cracked loodheramaun of a nephew.' Dinneen defines *liúdramán* as 'a lanky, lazy person'; Ó Dónaill adds, 'a loafer'. Fr Leo Morahan, who used to write a most informative article on local words in the Louisburgh, Co. Mayo, parish journal, *An Choinneal*, has this gloss: 'It is the correct name for the male of the honey bee. Social historians will be interested to note that the more common use of the word in Louisburgh is to indicate a fool. 'In other words, our ancestors equated the idler and the fool.'

The word *playsham* is used in many parts of Donegal, Mary Sweeney, formerly of Glenties, tells me. To her it means a foolish person. Patrick MacGill used it in like manner in *Glenmornan*: 'She's a plaisham, God help her.' Peadar O'Donnell used it imprecatively in *Islanders*: 'Plasham on you!' The Irish is *pléiseam*.

I recently heard a reference in a BBC radio programme to the American valedictions 'Have a good day' and 'Have a nice day', in which a listener expressed her regret that the use of the former phrase by, of all people, the Queen, was a typical example of the insidious effects of American popular culture on English speech. At a wedding I attended recently the priest let the phrase slip out and then apologised for using it.

Dear me, far from being a modern Americanism, the lovely valediction is at least 600 years old. In a macaronic carol written about 1400, the little birds rejoice on the morning of Christ's birth: 'Omnes gentes plaudite, I saw many birds sitting on a tree; They took their flight and flew away, With 'ego dixi, have a good day!'

Mary O'Mahony from Douglas, in Cork, wants to know the origin of *bastable*, a pot oven in which bread is made. The answer is kindly supplied by David Hopkinson, who lives at Kinlough, Co. Leitrim: 'By chance, on Friday I had looked up Elizabeth David's description of small pot ovens in her *English Bread and Yeast Cookery* (there was a BBC radio programme on the subject). She tells how such ovens were a speciality of potteries in Barnstaple and thereabouts, and were exported to Wales, Ireland and early colonial America. So I imagine the ovens were named, in Ireland at least, from their source. (They were "in much repute in Devonshire and Cornwall and in the Welsh districts, and the bread baked in them is said to have a sweeter and more wholesome flavour than when baked in ordinary ovens," according to a writer in 1883.)'

Many of the words connected with food have interesting pedigrees. Take *omelette*. It came to us in the 17th century from the French *omelette*, changed from *alumette*, from *alumelle*, the blade of a sword. This *alumelle*, in its turn, was changed by mistaken division from *la lamelle*, from Latin *lamella*, diminutive of *lamina*, a thin plate of metal. The omelette, then, was so called because of its thin, flat shape; and the French, in making a hash of things, gave English a beautiful word.

Nancy Reich from Orlando, Florida, bought a *báinín* jumper recently. She knows where *báinín* comes from, thanks to an Internet friend in Bord Fáilte; it's the *jumper* that's causing her problems. Well, *jumper* can be traced back to the Arabic *jubbah*, a long, loose linen coat adopted by the Crusaders from the Saracen. By the 17th century the word had become *jump*, and it was chiefly used of a short coat worn by Presbyterian ministers. A century later, Dr Johnson defines it as 'a waistcoat worn by sickly ladies.' The longer word *jumper* first appeared in 1853; it was a garment worn by sailors, and did not become fashionable until this century, when women decided that it looked quite well on them too, especially when worn nice and tight.

Two queries from C.J. Slator of Hawthornden Road, Belfast. When he was a small boy and came home with his socks down over his boots, his grandmother used to say, 'You're like an old munchie.' *Munchie*, common enough in placenames in the north, is the Irish *móinteach*, mossland, moorland. She was calling young Master Slator a bogman.

His second word is *staughy*, not found in the dictionaries and thus important as well as being elusive. *Staughy* is a mixture of leftovers: 'Are we having a staughy for tea to-night?' This, I'm pretty sure, is from the Irish *stác*, defined by O'Reilly's dictionary as 'offal'.

## Stelling and Hother

Bill Colfer from Slade, that delightful little fishing village in the Hook Peninsula in Co. Wexford, is director of the Norman Connection, a conference that takes place in Fethard-on-Sea every September. On one of those days yours truly will be blathering about words collected by a schoolmaster over a century ago a bit further east along the coast and sent to Dublin for appraisal. The antiquarian who examined the manuscript, Joseph Lloyd, thought highly of it, but he died before he could get it published. It lay in a drawer until somebody went to work on its extensive mutilation more than sixty years ago. I've been trying to sort the thing out.

Anyway, Mr Colfer sent me an interesting word they have in the Hook (Co. Wexford), and I hope I have solved the problem of its origin for him. The word is *stellan* and it means a stone shelf in an alcove on which the water bucket was kept. The word, I must confess, was new to me.

It is not found as Mr Colfer has it in the dialect dictionaries, but I'm pretty sure it's related to *steel*, a prop, support; a stand or framework to support barrels, a word found in northern England and in Scotland. There is also a verb *stell*, which means to place, set, fix. The word is from Old English *stellan*, to place, set.

'Should Mr Colfer's word, a noun, be spelled *stellin(g)*? I think so. The *ing* suffix often formed nouns from verbs. Think of the second coming; meeting; a wedding; winnings.

To *hother* is used by an 80-year-old man who lives in Waterford city, Mary Walsh from Ferrybank tells me. This is how her old acquaintance uses the word: 'I can still hother down to the pub and hother back again on me own, thank God.' The good lady asks me if her friend is confusing *hother* with *totter*, an old word that comes from Middle English *toter*, swing, corresponding to Old English *tealtrean,* to stagger, by the way.

From Flemish, *hotteren*, to totter, shake, this. Words from Flemish in the English of Ireland are scarce. But we shouldn't jump to the conclusion that this interesting word came with Fitzstephens's archers and artisans all those years ago. It is common in many of the dialects of English and may have come to Waterford port in later times.


## Stillion – Fecket – Caddie

I am grateful to many readers for informing me that Billy Colfer's Slade word *stellin(g)* is found in many places as *stillion*. Madge Anderson of Trees Road, Mount Merrion, Dublin, remembers her Limerick mother's stillion, 'a timber bench or form, pronounced *furrum* (because of Irish *fuarma*). On it stood the milk chums to be sent to the creamery the following day.' I now have the word from Clare, Tipperary, north Kilkenny and west Waterford. Thanks, too, all who wrote reminding me that Irish has borrowed the word as *stillín,* and especially to a hussy who signed her letter 'Martina'. 'I'm worried about you,' she says. 'You need to eat more fish, and to down a few more taoscáns every night. Your brain obviously needs nurture and lubrication. You explained the origin of the word to us in UCD back in the eighties, you know, and told us that it came from *stell*, with *ing* added to make a noun of it, as you told Mr Colfer.' That's the thanks you get.

James Hannon from Larne asks about the word *fecket.* It is a word he has heard many times in Scotland, particularly in Ayr; he has not come across it in Ulster. The word means both a waistcoat and a cardigan. Fecket can also mean a vest, or a *simmet,* to use the

Ulster word. Burns has 'Grim loon! he gat me by the fecket' in his *Poem to Mr Mitchell*. Origin a mystery. A *fir-fecket* was, and probably still is, a coffin in Burns's country.

*Fecket* has not, apparently, been recorded in Ulster; C.I. Macafee's *Ulster Dialect Dictionary* doesn't have it. *Simmet* is very common. This seems to be used only of a man's vest, or a baby's. It is a Scots word and may have come directly from Old French *samit*, a silk undergarment.

A French import which has since travelled the world from Scotland is *caddie*. From French *cadet*, the youngest son, caddies were once sent by the noble families of Scotland to serve as attendants in other great houses. The lady who wrote this never played golf, I fancy: 'Where will I get a little foot-page, Where will I get a caddie, That will run swift to bonnie Aboyne, Wi' a letter to my rantin' laddie?'

## The French Influence on Scots

The ancient friendship between Scotland and France which lasted from the time of Edward III down to the fall of the Jacobites was bound to leave a mark on Scots, and consequently on the English of Ulster. I must thank the anonymous Ulsterwoman who sent me a present of Isabel Sinclair's lexicon of Franco-Scottish words, published at the beginning of the present century: thank you kindly, ma'm.

A fascinating little book this *Thistle and Fleur de Lys* is. I have tried out many of the words it contains on northern friends of mine and they were amazed at how many of these are still in use in greater Ulster, as I heard it recently described on UTV. Many of these words have escaped the net of Macafee's dictionary, which contains 15,000 entries. Here's a sampling.

*Coclico*: Red. 'A coclico ribbon'. From *coquelicot*, the poppy. Still heard in north-west Donegal. *Howtowdy*: A pullet. Graham's *Social Life in Scotland* had a description of Adam Smith dining in a tavern on hen broth, composed of two or three howtowdies and haggis. Old French *huteaudeau*. The Cardinal de Lorraine told

Queen Mary that Darnley was 'un gentil huteaudeau', and to treat him with contempt. *Howtowdy* is still used aboo Churchill in Donegal by ceoboys describing young women. *Jelly*: Cold, haughty. 'Leave off your pride, jelly Janet; use it not any mair.' From *gelée*, frost. A friend has heard 'The wun 'ud jell ye to the bone' at the back of Errigal.

*Mange*: A meal. 'I saw the hurcheon and the hare In hiddlings hirple here and there To mak' their morning mange.' From *manger*, food. Many years ago Peter Byrne, a schoolteacher from Tacumshane, Co. Wexford, God rest him now, took down this word from a fisherman from Kilkeel, Co. Down. *Hurcheon*, a hedgehog is another French word in disguise: *hérisson*, from Latin *ericius*. In Donegal as *urchin* as well.

*To cooter* is still in common use by knitters in parts of Co. Donegal. It means to knit carelessly. From *coudre*, to sew, stitch. *Jupe* is another word you'll hear sometimes from Antrim and Donegal women. To Sinclair it's a skirt; to a Donegal woman I know it's a slip. French *jupe*, a skirt, petticoat, slip. Macafee has this one.

And lastly, the Scots delicacy *haggis*. Origin unknown, says Oxford. Perhaps from *haggen*, to hack, says Collins. From French *hachis*, minced meat, says Sinclair. What are you having yourself?

## Durn – Mooch – Mitch

Hurling goalkeepers are people apart, agile as cats, courageous as toreros, so I have no intention of disparaging the breed by telling you where I recently heard one of them described as a *durn*, except to say it was at a club match somewhere in the southeast. My companion was worried about his team's goalie; like you-know-who he stoppeth one of three, and that on a good day, I was told.

'Look at him, rooted to the ground like a bloody durn,' my friend exclaimed when goal number four went in. Certainly, he was no Tony Reddan, the best I've ever seen. I sense that my companion would not just then have appreciated an inquiry as to the meaning and etymology of *durn*; later he explained that a *durn* was the pillar of a gate.

Since then I have heard that the word was once common in north Co. Dublin, where it meant the jamb of a door. The dialect dictionaries of England tell me the word is common there, especially in the southern counties, and in Yorkshire too. There are a variety of regional variants, *dorn, darn, dearn, doorn* among them. I'm sure the word has a Norse origin; Swedish has *dymi,* a door-post.

Gerry McCarthy, of Botanic Road, Glasnevin, tells me his mother, a north Cork woman, used the word *mook* when she referred to a dim-wit.

I think the word has the same pedigree as *mooch,* a word as common across the water as it is here. *Mooch,* noun and verb, is from Norman French *mucher,* Old French *mucer,* to hide, secrete. Obviously its meaning has since been expanded, as has the meaning of *mitch.*

*Is mooch* related to *mitch? Mitch,* as well as to play truant from school, means, as does *mooch,* to idle. *Mitch* is from Old English *mycan,* to steal. But *mycan* and the French words I mentioned above probably have a common Germanic origin. Consider the Old High German *muhhan,* to prey upon.

*Mooching* and *mitching* have for centuries been connected with blackberries. Indeed, the dialect dictionaries tell me that in many parts of rural England *mooch* and *moocher, mitch* and *mitcher,* are common words both for blackberries and those who pick them, so that Falstaff, when he says: 'Shall the blessed sun of heaven prove a micher and eat blackberries?', was referring not to truancy but to a picker of the luscious fruit of the humble bramble, Irish *dris.*


## Thought Your Latin Was Rusty?

One or two curious spirits asked me during the recent election campaign where the word *candidate* came from. It is from the Latin *candidus,* white. Those intending to claim the suffrages of the people in ancient Rome were obliged to dress up in white togas, being therefore called *candidati.*

Candidates are known to have *ambition* but perhaps not all of them knew that this word is also from the Latin, through Old French. The Latin *ambitio* meant a going round of candidates, striving to please, of course, from *ambire*, to go round. Milton had the old meaning of the word in mind when he wrote: 'To reign is worth ambition, though in hell.'

One of my local candidates claimed in his election literature to have worked assiduously for the good of all. A local man to whom I spoke about our friend's chances said he would not vote for him because sitting on his *bundún* was all he had done for years back, in his humble opinion. Interestingly, *assiduously* comes from another Latin word *assiduus*, sitting down to (something), on one's *bundún*, where else?; from *assidere*, to sit beside, from *sedere*, to sit.

Whatever about being assiduous, our candidate must have been attentive to the needs of his electors; once again he was successful. Attentive comes from Latin *attendere*, from *ad*, a prefix meaning to express motion to, direction towards, and *tendere*, to stretch. I can see the old Roman polician sitting in his white *toga*, his *tabula* in his hand, the butt of a *stilus* at the ready, stretching out his neck to listen to the complaint of a potential *suffragator*, *ebrius* as a skunk, who just might give him his *votum* if he bought him another few scoops of *vinum*. Thought your Latin was rusty, did you?

A man who knows the sea, having fished from all the great ports from Killybegs to Vigo in his time, asks me where the word *dorm*, a catnap, comes from; he has heard it used by seafarers from Yarmouth, the Faroes, Shetland and Orkney.

Well, it didn't come directly from the Latin *dormire*, to sleep, I feel sure, but from a language that has left a more lasting impression on the speech of seamen from the northern world. Old Norse, borrowing from Latin, has *dorma*, a snooze; and the word can still be heard in modern Iceland as well as in Killybegs among the old-timers, according to one of them, my friend, Tom Carr.


## Celebrating the Christmas


'I'd love to be going home for the Christmas,' said a friend from Cheshire to me the other evening. He's been in Ireland a long time, and I thought he had picked up the definite article here, where it is a relic of the Irish, *an* Nollaig. I mentioned it to him. 'The Christmas is used all over rural England,' he said. 'Check it out.' I did. He is right.

This is from Shropshire: 'such a thing happened,' the folk say, 'in the Christmas' ... 'one special care was in putting away any suds for washing purposes; it was most unlucky to keep them in the house during the Christmas.'

The English made a verbal noun of Christmas – *Christmasing.*

You'll find it in various guises. In Wordsworth's special place it still means coming home for the Christmas holidays: 'I see that Mary's *kermassing.*' In Surrey Christmasing meant to go about collecting the Christmas presents. Christmasing in old London meant selling any evergreen used for decoration. Mayhew (the 19th-century one) has: 'There is a large trade done in Christmasing.'

In Cornwall the word still means a Christmas present. My little grand-daughter phoned me from there a month ago to remind me not to forget her Christmasing.

'The Christmas' in her part of the world was a special cake made on Christmas Eve. *Notes and Queries* had this to say about it back in 1878: 'The peculiarity of the cake is that a small portion of the dough in the centre of the top of each is pulled up and made into a form which resembles a very small cake on the top of a large one, and this centre-piece is specially called "the Christmas". Each person in the house has his or her special cake.'

They have their *Bloc na Nollag*, too, in Cornwall, the Yule log, only they call it the *Christmas Mock*. Why I don't know, but it may have something to do with the figure of a man they draw on the block before burning it.

In Dorset the *Christmas Sheaf* is still given to cattle on Christmas morning. The stables and byres are decorated with *Christ's Thorn* – the original Christmas tree, the holly. They say the crown of thorns was made from it.

Do any of these words and traditions sound familiar to you? I'm sure they do. In some respects, we are not native here, or anywhere, as John Hewitt said.

Anyway, as the old people used to say where I come from, a happy Christenmas to you all.

# Index